HOW TO PLAY
the HARMONICA

and Other Life Lessons

SAM BARRY

GIBBS SMITH
TO ENRICH AND INSPIRE HUMANKIND
Salt Lake City | Charleston | Santa Fe | Santa Barbara

First Edition
13 12 11 10 09   5 4 3 2 1

To Kathi

Text © 2009 Sam Barry
Illustration on page 25 © Remie Geoffroi

Published by
Gibbs Smith
P.O. Box 667
Layton, Utah 84041

Orders: 1.800.835.4993
www.gibbs-smith.com

Designed by Stephanie Orma
Printed and bound in Canada
Gibbs Smith books are printed on either recycled, 100% post-consumer
waste, FSC-certified papers or on paper produced from a
100% certified sustainable forest/controlled wood source.

Library of Congress Cataloging-in-Publication Data

Barry, Sam.
  How to play the harmonica : and other life lessons / Sam Barry. — 1st ed.
    p. cm.
  ISBN-13: 978-1-4236-0570-6
  ISBN-10: 1-4236-0570-5
  1. Harmonica—Instruction and study. 2. Harmonica—Humor. I. Title.
  MT682.B39 2009
  788.8'2193—dc22
                              2009003344

Contents ♪

Foreword to MY LITTLE BROTHER SAM'S BOOK —By Dave Barry

I HAVE KNOWN MY LITTLE BROTHER SAM SINCE he was born, and I can state for a fact that he has always been an amazing person. At the age of five he was already composing classical music.

No, wait, I'm thinking of Mozart. But Sam was definitely a fun little brother, exactly the right height to administer a noogie to. And he grew into a fun grown-up, the perfect person to write a book about playing. Sam has always been playful. Oh, he has done a few serious things in his life. For a while he was—I am not making this up—a Presbyterian minister in Omaha. But he was a *playful* Presbyterian minister. It would not surprise me if, in his day, he was considered the most playful Presbyterian minister in the entire state of Nebraska, assuming there are rankings.

Another thing about Sam is that he is highly musical. He and I belong to a rock band called the Rock Bottom Remainders, which is made up mostly of authors, including Stephen King, Amy Tan, Mitch Albom, Ridley Pearson, Kathi Goldmark, Scott Turow, Roy Blount Jr., Greg Iles, and Matt Groening. The plan in forming this band was to gather together a group of authors with musical talent and raise money for good causes. The only flaw in this plan was that most of the authors don't *have* any musical talent. Our genre was best described by Roy Blount as "hard listening music." We sound like people using amplified instruments to demolish a shed.

But Sam is one of the few shining lights in the band. He is a very good harmonica and keyboard player; in fact, for a while, when he was not in his wacky Presbyterian-minister phase, he was a professional musician. Not only is he musically talented, but he has an amazing ability to transfer his musicality to other people.

For example, I once wrote a song about Tupperware called *The Tupperware Blues*. At the risk of sounding vain, I am going to state that this song became, over the years, one of the better-known blues songs about Tupperware, and eventually it came to the attention of the folks at Tupperware World Headquarters in Kissimmee, Florida, who asked me to come up there and perform it at a convention of Tupperware distributors. Naturally, I said yes. An opportunity like that comes along once in a lifetime, if that.

Anyway, *The Tupperware Blues* has an important harmonica part, so I asked my editor at the time, Gene Weingarten, if he would

FACT: Mozart was **never** asked to play at Tupperware World Headquarters.

accompany me. The problem was that, although Gene owned a harmonica, he did not, technically, know how to play it. Gene has no natural musical talent. He is so musically untalented that—and I do not make this statement lightly—he could belong to the Remainders. All he could do with his harmonica was blow into it in a way that upset his dog.

So I had Gene call my brother Sam in California, and Sam taught Gene, in one lesson via long distance, to play *The Tupperware Blues*. When we performed for the Tupperware distributors, they gave us a standing ovation. Of course, they also gave a standing ovation to a set of ovenware. But that is not my point. My point is that Sam, thanks to his amazing ability, was able to administer a musicality transfusion to my music-impaired friend *over the phone*.

I have seen Sam do the same thing many times with crowds. No matter how reserved people are, how timid, how insecure about their abilities, Sam can get them singing and stomping. It's a gift Sam has—the gift of making music, and getting others to make music, and having fun doing it. It's a gift he will share with you in this book.

This is not a book about learning to play the harmonica, exactly—although if you *want* to play the harmonica, this book will teach you. The real point of the book is what the title says—to learn how to play; or, more accurately, to *relearn* how to play, which is a skill we all have as kids but tend to lose as we age and develop jobs and responsibilities and gum problems. Sam's point is that you can get your playfulness back—that even in a grown-up world, you *can* play again; you *can* have fun.

So let him show you how. Read my little brother's book.

Or I will give you a noogie.

10

Acknowledgments

〜

I'D LIKE TO THANK MY SWEETHEART, Kathi Kamen Gold-mark, who learned how to play "Oh! Susanna" for this book; my amazing children Daniel and Laura, who continue to teach me how to play; and Tony and Marissa, who know how to play to the beat of their own drummer. I also want to thank my agent, Deb Warren, who remained playful and found this book a home. A big shout to my bandmates in the Rock Bottom Remainders, who don't know how to play music but do know how to play; to my bandmates in Los Train Wreck, who *do* know how to play music; to the sales guru Charles Boswell; to Eric Brandt and all my colleagues at HarperOne in San Francisco and HarperCollins in New York; and, of course, to the great team at Gibbs Smith, led by Gibbs, and my editor, Michelle Witte. Last, but not least, I want to thank my students over the years, who taught me much of what I am sharing in this book.

Prologue:
HOW PLAYING
CAN SAVE YOUR LIFE

LIGHTEN UP. YES, YOU. AND ME TOO.

We've all been taking ourselves far too seriously for too long, and as a result we've made a complete mess of things. Stress, fear, and anxiety rule our lives. Meanwhile, we're missing out on the most FUN-damental (I promise I won't do that again) joy of all. Human beings are hardwired to play, yet as we grow up that ability is often squashed by a regimented culture that respects conformity and control over spontaneity and joy. It's time we tapped into a gift every human (and every puppy) owns—one we're all born with—playfulness.

We have a choice. We can live life the regular old way or we can live it the playful way. More often than not the playful way will get us better results, and we will have more fun getting there.

For instance, we all know that it's a good idea to live with less stress in our lives, but—you might ask—how do we actually *do* this on a day-to-day basis?

Here are some examples of ordinary events that can be transformed into stress-reducers by doing them the Playful Way instead of the Regular Way.

Doing laundry the Regular Way:

1. Load washing machine with dirty clothes.
2. Measure and add soap.
3. Turn on machine.

Doing laundry the Playful Way:

1. Turn on your favorite music nice and loud.
2. Sing and dance along as you throw in an approximate amount of soap without measuring.
3. Remember the fun you had the last time you wore that silk teddy (this works for women, too), and make a mental note to send a sexy e-mail to the person you were with.

Taking the kids to school the Regular Way:

1. Yell at everyone that they're going to be late and make you late for work, until someone (probably you) is on the verge of tears or putting his fist through a wall.
2. In the car, lecture your children about being late—and while

you're at it you can bring up the subject of their filthy rooms, their bad grades, and their slacker friends.

3. Keep the radio tuned to a station that specializes in news of really scary world events.

4. Neglect to notice the forgotten lunch box/homework/backpack until you are miles away and late for work.

Taking the kids to school the Playful Way:

1. Offer a treat or special privilege for the first one standing at the door, ready to go.

2. Tune the radio to a station your kids like and dance (with both hands on the wheel) and sing along at top volume. You get extra points if your singing embarrasses any teenagers who happen to be in the car—they need to learn to lighten up too.

3. When you get to school, tell your kids that today you're going to trade places—they'll go to work for you and you'll learn algebra from Ms. Hoffbutter.

※ ※ ※ ※ ※ ※ ※ ※ ※ ※

"Great," you the reader are now saying, "another self-help book that offers patently obvious advice and pretends it's new and profound and is completely out of touch with how we really live." Never fear! This is no ordinary self-help book. We have a secret weapon, one that the Pentagon has been keeping under wraps for fear that one of our enemies or, even worse, the Congress of the United States, might get hold of it. I'm talking, of course, about the harmonica.

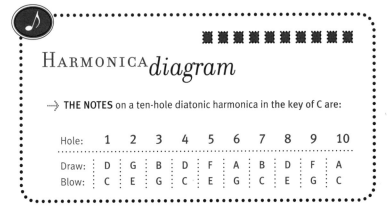

HARMONICA *diagram*

···> **THE NOTES** on a ten-hole diatonic harmonica in the key of C are:

Hole:	1	2	3	4	5	6	7	8	9	10
Draw:	D	G	B	D	F	A	B	D	F	A
Blow:	C	E	G	C	E	G	C	E	G	C

There are books that teach you how to play the harmonica, and there are countless self-help books about how to improve your attitude, reduce stress, and enjoy life. What's missing is a book that combines these elements. Here's a typical conversation you might hear at the water cooler:

Co-worker #1: I'm feeling so stressed. I wish I could enjoy life more.
Co-worker #2: I wish I knew how to play the harmonica!

Start playing the harmonica and those extra pounds will melt away. Your spirits will lift, and your life will be smooth and well-organized. Smokers will quit smoking, old people will feel young again, and young people will discover the meaning of life. Aches and pains, self-doubt, and nagging worries will be a thing of yesterday. You will make peace with your deadbeat brother-in-law, your golf game will improve, and you'll find true love. Your salary will double and double again and you will be inundated with fabulous career choices. That toilet that won't stop running will run no more. Continue to play and the world will experience an unprecedented era of peace and prosperity. And all because we're learning to play.

HOW CAN THIS POSSIBLY BE?
INSTEAD OF ANSWERING THIS QUESTION,
LET'S LOOK AT SEVERAL IMPORTANT
REASONS *why* YOU SHOULD LEARN TO PLAY
THE HARMONICA:

1. It will make you a little happier. You will discover new ways to have fun, and most of us need more fun in our lives.
2. The harmonica is unpretentious. You can even play it in your underwear. You can also play it in someone else's underwear.
3. It's inexpensive and low-tech. There's not much point in standing around with your buddies staring at your harmonica, admiring its curves and shine and discussing what year it was made. No—it's all about the music.
4. Playing the harmonica will force you to let go of preconceived notions about music, art, performance, status, accomplishment, appearances, formality, beauty, and education.
5. I don't have a fifth point to make, but it looks good to have more than four of these.

█ █ █ █ █ █ █ █ █ █

You don't need a special talent to learn to play the harmonica. You don't need an exceptional sense of melody, or rhythm, or fabulous wind power. You don't need to read music or understand music theory. All you need is the desire and a harmonica. Passionate emotions like desire sometimes get a bad rap because we think they might get us in trouble. But desire is also a sure sign of vitality.

If we don't have the desire to learn new things, it's time to check our pulse. A lack of desire means we need to get out more, see the world, meet new people, and try new things. But the fact that you're reading a book on how to play is a good sign. You're in the game. And remember, this is a game—we are doing this for pure fun. No one will ever grade you and there will never be a test.

I play this magical, pocket-sized gizmo because it enables me to instantly make music straight from my heart. There is no requirement to join an elite club, but many times I've been able to join a circle of musicians and add my part to the music. The harmonica allows me to make art without it being a Very Serious Thing.

So pick up a harmonica and start fooling around. Now, stop it! Get back to work!

No, really, just let yourself have fun. Let's start breathing through this delightful contraption and be transported to a simpler, gentler world.

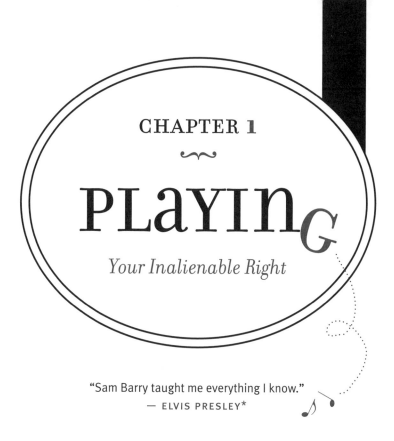

CHAPTER 1

PLAYING

Your Inalienable Right

"Sam Barry taught me everything I know."
— ELVIS PRESLEY*

HOWARD LOVED TO SING. HE JOINED THE GLEE CLUB
at his school—partly to meet girls, but mostly because he really loved
music. At the first rehearsal, Howard was placed in the back because
he was tall and because he was a bass. He was happily doing his best
to sing along with his fellow basses when the director banged his
baton on his music stand and shouted, "Stop!"

"You," he said, pointing directly at Howard. "Let me hear you
sing this part."

There are very few people who could have sung well in those
circumstances. Howard was not one of those very few. He tried to

* The author takes no responsibility for Mr. Presley's tragic demise.

sing, but what came out of his throat was a weird, tuneless warble. The conductor pointed his baton at Howard and announced, "You can't sing," in front of the whole choir—including the girls. Howard was mortified.

You may be saying, "Well, this conductor must have been a very cruel man." Or you may be wondering how bad Howard's voice was. To answer the second question first, Howard has a good, regular-guy voice. There was no valid reason to tell him he couldn't sing. As for the conductor being cruel, I have heard similar stories often enough to know that this phenomenon of telling people they can't sing/dance/play isn't just about a few mean adults. What is it about? It's about adults losing their own sense of play and imagination.

Howard found his voice despite the discouragement and went on to become one of the greatest baseball players of all time. No, really, Howard used his voice in another way by becoming a minister. But Howard, and millions of others like him, went through life afraid of doing what he should have been able to do naturally: sing. Somewhere along the way we forgot that the human spirit of creativity doesn't have to live up to the standards of show business or high art, neither of which leave much room for the everyday joy of self-expression. Lots of people have been shot down at a young age because someone decided they weren't good enough at something—music, art, sports, whatever—and so were told, in so many words, to sit down and shut up. It's time to reclaim the birthright of regular folks to be recreational singers, artists, performers, and brain surgeons.

If you don't already own one, I suggest you buy a scalpel. No, wait, I mean a ten-hole major diatonic harmonica. The Japanese company Tombo has a line of well-made harmonicas named after Lee Oskar, the Copenhagen-born harmonicist who was a founding member of the band War. Hohner makes many good, reasonably priced models: the Golden Melody is one; the Special 20 is another. If you're a purist, you can buy

a Hohner Marine Band, which has a wooden comb. Marine Band harmonicas come in a box with a picture of a bunch of Marines—presumably the band. There's a romance about this model, but you should be aware that the wood has a tendency to swell up. There are numerous other good, reasonably priced harps available, but one of

HARMONICA *lesson* #1

⋯⟩ **EACH DIATONIC HARMONICA IS BUILT IN A PARTICULAR KEY.** (If you want to learn more about keys right away, see page 22.) A C-major diatonic harmonica (or C "harp," as they are often called) is designed to play tones only from the C major scale. If you're playing "Oh! Susanna" on a C harp, the song will be in the key of C. Do the same thing on an A harp and now the song is in the key of A—change the harmonica and the key is changed for you. Pretty cool, huh? That's why the harmonica is the people's instrument. But if you're not ready to buy more than one harmonica, don't worry; you only need one ten-hole harmonica in any key to begin learning, and anything you learn on one will work on another harp in a different key.

these is a good start. If you can afford more than one, buy a few different models until you figure out which model you like best.

Buying your harmonica the Regular Way:

1. Go to a music store.
2. Ask the clerk for a harmonica.
3. Buy the harmonica.

Buying your harmonica the Playful Way:

1. Put on a 1940s-era zoot suit and dark sunglasses, slick back your hair, and saunter into the nearest blues club. Men, there's no reason you can't try this too.
2. Talk to the harmonica player about his instrument during a break.
3. After you sober up (remember, don't drink and drive) download some Sonny Terry and Brownie McGhee songs to listen to on your way to the music store.
4. When you get to the music store, head to the drum section and start banging on everything in sight. Try out the guitars and the keyboards. Be sure to crank up the volume.
5. When you've got everyone's attention, head over to the counter and buy a harmonica.

Hold your harmonica in your hand and take a look at it. If what you are seeing is a small knife, you took that joke about brain surgery too seriously and you should get back on your meds. Most ten-hole harmonicas have the holes numbered 1 through 10, starting with the hole on the far left, the lowest notes, labeled one, and the hole on the far right, the highest notes, labeled ten. Lightly blow on all the holes, from number 1 through number 10. Now try sliding from 1 to 10 and back down again. Now try drawing (inhaling) through a hole. Notice that it's a different note. (See diagram, page 14.)

Keep breathing in and out through your harmonica, moving up and down and exploring the instrument to see what sounds it makes. Notice the difference between high and low, in and out, soft breathing and hard breaths. Are you feeling dizzy? Isn't this fun? Talk into the harmonica. You are already playing. If you never did

HARMONICA *lesson* #2

····> **DRAW (THAT IS, BREATHE IN)** on hole 1 and slide to hole number 10. Even if the holes on your harmonica aren't labeled, this is how we will keep track of where you are as you learn. I will indicate which hole or holes I want you to play with numbers for the holes with a down arrow (↓) for inhale and an up arrow (↑) for exhale. Think of the up arrow as pointing away from you, or blowing out, and the down arrow as toward you, or inhaling. It's a little cumbersome, but we need some way to communicate about what to play. However—and this is important—long-term, you will probably want to play the harmonica without the use of any form of notation. Whether this means you will learn to improvise or memorize songs or just fool around depends on your style and interests. But either way, the diatonic harmonica is not an instrument where reading music plays a large role. In other words, you don't have to learn to read music. Isn't that great? Instead, you should strive to learn and play by ear, even if this simply means being able to memorize a song and know when you are hitting a wrong note. Learn to trust your ear, even if you are convinced that you don't have one. I promise that you do—you were just discouraged from using it long ago by Howard's teacher.

anything more, you have already made music. (Isn't that a great cop-out for me?)

I invite you to jump into the party, which will be a very noisy and strange party if everyone is a harmonica player wearing a zoot suit. Right from the beginning it's a great idea to try playing along with recorded music or any music you hear. I knew one guy who learned a lot by playing along with television ads. If an ice cream truck comes to your neighborhood, try playing along with the jingle. But don't play the harmonica while you're eating the ice cream. Also, since music comes in different keys, you may not have the right-key harmonica for every song. If you're patient and you keep trying, you'll find a song that suits your harmonica. I learned a lot about what keys are and how music works just muddling through, making mistakes, playing along with songs when I didn't have the right harp, trying to figure out tunes by ear. You have to be brave and let yourself play lots of wrong notes. And again, if you buy a few harmonicas in different keys, that helps.

HARMONICA*lesson* #3

┈┈➤ **I HOPE ALL OF THIS TALK ABOUT KEYS** isn't sounding too technical and scary. It's a concept that, once grasped, is helpful for playing music. A key is seven tones in fixed relationship to one of the tones, rather like home base. Think of Julie Andrews singing the "do-re-mi" scale in *The Sound of Music*—"do" is the primary tone the others relate to and to which the song returns. We'll try playing this "do-re-mi" scale with Julie a little later.

It's interesting to think of the other meanings of "key"—the key that opens a door, the key to a map, the keystone of a building. Understanding keys in music will help you understand why some notes sound good when you are playing along with a song, while others sound terrible. Scales can serve as an entryway and guide to music once we begin playing. Most people think of scales as being really boring, but they don't have to be. Musicians who play hot leads and beautiful lines are usually also musicians who know something about scales. But if learning scales really puts you off, don't despair—for you, there are songs you can learn that serve the same purpose. For

Harmonica *lesson* #4

····⟩ **NOW WE NEED TO LEARN HOW TO HOLD A HARMONICA.** First of all, you should be wearing the correct clothing. For men, a tuxedo is *de rigueur,* while women have more choices—a bikini, a teddy, or nothing at all. Oh, I'm sorry, that's the dress code for a James Bond movie. When you're playing the harmonica you can wear anything you want. I live in San Francisco, where men wear the teddies. When it comes to holding the harmonica, you can pretty much hold it any way that works. The legendary country blues artist Sonny Terry famously played his harmonica "upside down," with the high notes to the left, and he was pretty darned good. There is really no *one* required way to hold your harmonica, but here's what I would suggest:

First, you're going to have to put down your martini. Now, place the harp between your left-hand thumb and your index and middle fingers, lightly pinching the harp between your thumb and the end of your two fingers around 8, 9, and 10, the three holes that make the highest notes (number 1 is on your left and number 10 on your right). Now
····⟩

HARMONICA*lesson* #4 *(continued)*

you have a harmonica sandwich. Your pointer finger and thumb should be toward the back of the harp to allow your lips to go over it—you're going to be putting the instrument deeper in your mouth than you think.

Hold the four fingers on your left hand flat and together. **The job of your left hand is to move the harmonica left and right to change notes. Your right hand's job is to help make a chamber to play into that makes the sound richer and warmer.** Place the palm of your right hand against the back side of your left hand and pinkie to make a cup around the back of the harp. You want the back of your harmonica to be in a little pitch-black room made by your hands, with no light coming in from the bottom or top or side. When you play you can pull your right hand away a little, breaking the seal of the cup, to make a "wah wah" sound. Also, the cupping itself, whether fully airtight or not, makes your tone warmer, much as the wooden body of a guitar makes the vibrating string sound richer.

instance, the beginning of the song "Joy to the World" is the major scale descending, and the famous lead-guitar line on the Temptations' "My Girl" is the major pentatonic scale. (This handy scale is simply the major scale with two notes left out: fa and ti. So the scale is do, re, mi, so, la—a five-note scale. If you play only the black notes on the piano, you're playing this scale. In addition to "My Girl," it also sounds a lot like Chinese classical music.) In music, as in life, there's always a playful, creative way to get the job done.

Now, let's do some playing. I will use the terms "blow" and "draw" to indicate which direction you are breathing through the harmonica because saying "blow" and "suck" over and over again could get this book banned. Play one long breath in and one long breath out, listening to how it sounds different each way. Does it sound like there's

a leak anywhere? Try to maintain a seal by sticking the harp deep enough inside your mouth so that the wet, fleshy parts of your lips are touching the metal. Ooh baby, this is better than kissing, huh? Now carefully place the rubber chicken on the crown of your head. Just kidding! The rubber chicken goes down your pants. But you do need to get the harmonica farther in your mouth than you think. A doctor student of mine told me that this line between the dry and wet part of our lips is called the vermillion border. You have to get the harmonica past the vermillion border, which sounds to me a little like the title of a porn film, thriller, or perhaps a sewing pattern.

About now you may be thinking that's all fine, but how the heck do I make a single note? Or maybe you've stopped reading? Maybe you're at the supermarket juggling oranges for your children's amusement, in which case you've gotten the whole point of this book already. Although I'd like to point out that your kids, being in their twenties, ought to get out of the shopping cart and go find jobs. Anyhow, I know you want to play some songs, and you will. But the first step is getting to know your instrument. Feel it, breathe through it, and listen to it, unless it's telling you to do something you shouldn't. There *are* recorded instances of demon-possessed harmonicas. If it's a nice harmonica, take it out to dinner, maybe go to a movie—perhaps *The Vermillion Border*, the new pornographic thriller. Don't rush the courtship.

The method I would suggest for creating a single note is something like what people do when they whistle (don't worry, you don't need to know how to whistle). But first, to hear what a single note sounds like, use your fingers to block everything except a single hole. Now lightly blow and draw through that hole. Listen to the sound it makes. Are you hearing only one note? If you are still getting more than one, make sure you have a seal on the other holes, and breathe more gently.

Obviously we can't play the harmonica with our fingers in our mouths. We also can't play the harmonica with anyone else's fingers in our mouths. Try this: open your mouth wide enough to cover three holes. Now rest the harp inside your mouth on your lower lip, tilting it so the holes are pointing slightly down, with your upper lip halfway over the top cover. Try to guide a steady airstream into the middle of the three holes, as if you are whistling into the harmonica. Don't force this, and stay relaxed—it may take some time to consistently play a single note. If your notes sound breathy it probably means your lips aren't making a good seal, and you should place the harp a little deeper in your mouth. It's okay—in fact, it's necessary—to get saliva on your harp so it can move it around more easily. In other words, drool is as necessary in playing the harmonica as it is in Senate hearings.

Don't worry about your harmonica becoming tarnished. I've always loved the way the covers of my harps aged, the metal becoming discolored and mottled over time. Using my harps makes them mine more than by paying the purchase price. We all have things in our lives that we treasure for their familiarity and history—an old sweatshirt that feels just right, a pair of perfectly broken-in shoes, that suitcase of unmarked one hundred dollar bills you have stashed in your closet. Over time my harmonicas become old friends, and even when they are worn out I don't throw them away. Open any closet in my house and harmonicas will come tumbling down on your head.

HARMONICA *lesson* #5

⋯⟩ **NOW LET'S TRY PLAYING A SINGLE NOTE.**

Place the harmonica in your mouth and lightly blow on hole number 1: $\overset{1}{\underset{\uparrow}{}}$

Now draw on the same hole: $\overset{1}{\underset{\downarrow}{}}$

Drawing (that is, breathing in) slowly through the harmonica on these lower notes can be a little unwieldy. Keep your mouth as relaxed as possible, under the circumstances, and breathe in gently. If the notes sound flat or sour (a common experience for beginners), you should try opening your nose so you are breathing in through both the harp and your nose at the same time. Now see if you can hold a honeydew melon between your knees.

Now I'm going to toss something harder at you—a watermelon!—no, seriously, the major scale. Don't worry about getting it or any of this just right, for now. If you are having trouble playing a single note, just keep trying, and don't give yourself a hard time if other notes creep in. Our goal is always to make progress, not to be perfect. For example, it would be great if I could come up with a really clever or funny thing to say here, but I can't, so instead I'll just say it directly—perfectionism kills people. By demanding perfection of ourselves we deny our own humanity. No one—repeat, NO ONE—except Mary Poppins is perfect, and perfection is not the goal. Instead, it is the willingness to try that we should celebrate.

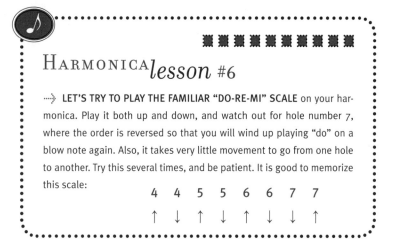

HARMONICA *lesson* #6

···⟩ **LET'S TRY TO PLAY THE FAMILIAR "DO-RE-MI" SCALE** on your harmonica. Play it both up and down, and watch out for hole number 7, where the order is reversed so that you will wind up playing "do" on a blow note again. Also, it takes very little movement to go from one hole to another. Try this several times, and be patient. It is good to memorize this scale:

4	4	5	5	6	6	7	7
↑	↓	↑	↓	↑	↓	↓	↑

The first harmonica I ever owned was a hand-me-down, ten-hole, major diatonic instrument that was given to me by my brother Phil. It's the kind of harmonica you've seen a million times, and it's the kind you should use with this book. Phil was passing the harmonica on to me in the casual way of siblings, just as brother Dave passed on bicycle-riding skills and sister Katy passed along a song.

I immediately liked the folksy sounds my new harmonica made, which reminded me of old, scratchy recordings of people playing songs about hard times. Because I was young, I had no fear of sounding incompetent. Isn't that great? I got in the habit of playing when I was out walking, fooling around with noises and exploring the sounds of this small instrument. In a way, I was unconsciously using the harmonica as a tool for meditation, breathing in and out, slowly, softly, deeply, shaping my mouth to see how it changed the sound, checking out what was grating, what was pretty, and what sounded like music to my ears. Gradually I learned to "speak" through the harmonica, working my tongue, singing with my breath through the reeds of the harp rather than my vocal chords.

No doubt to a passerby I sounded like what I was, a kid blowing and sucking air through a harmonica he hadn't yet learned how to play. But I didn't really care. I knew I didn't have it down yet, but I was willing to dive in and keep trying, dreaming of the day when I could play beautifully. It certainly helped that I didn't have a choir director telling me I wasn't any good and that, therefore, I should forever shut up.

You **don't** have to be young to learn.

We can have new adventures at any time of life. Unfortunately, as we take on the responsibilities of adulthood, our fear of appearing silly or inept or less accomplished in the eyes of others increases and we shy away from trying anything new. We allow these concerns to dictate our behavior and miss a great deal. The only way to overcome our fear is to turn off or ignore the external and internal voices that say "no you can't," and go for it. I know—easier said than done. Personally, I use beer, but there are some unfortunate side effects—like, how come I woke up with a large pair of men's boxer shorts on my head? And where's my car? And where am I?

Back when I was walking in the woods playing the harmonica, I wasn't worried about how I measured up against someone else, or how I sounded, or if I was using my time and energy wisely. I was Huck Finn on an adventure, and I just wanted to play. I wanted to make some of my own music. In a safe place, open to the desire, I was able to make the connection between the sounds my breath made passing through the reeds of the harmonica and the possibility of creating beauty. I found a way to tap into something powerful—call it soul—that was in me, but way beyond me.

How do we get in touch with this power? First of all, put a bagel on your head and start having fun. Not the kind of fun that is forced upon us by overbearing professional motivators and bad wedding singers (I mean the singers are bad, not the weddings). And not brain-dead, passive fun—there's enough of that available through our televisions. We need to go for the old-fashioned kind of fun, the enjoyment that comes from creating something ourselves.

To do this, we need to reclaim our right to make our own music. In this passive society many of us have never grown any food or built or fixed anything. We no longer eat together in our own homes or play games face-to-face without computers intervening. We buy disposable, plastic stuff. We stare at the television and eat processed food. And the greatest crime of all is that we've stopped telling our own stories and making our own music. It's just plain wrong. We need to stop giving our brains and bodies over to entertainment that we sit and absorb like zombies. We need to start making some of our own noise again. We need to march on Washington, D.C., by the millions with underwear on our heads!

For a few dollars and without any electricity, you can make your own song today. You can *play*. You need to play, in every sense. And the world needs you to play. So, get a harmonica and start fooling around. Go somewhere private and huff and puff and toot and bleat and screech until you've got some idea of what you're holding in your hand. (Hopefully it's not someone else's underwear.) Play it soft and play it loud, play it high and play it low. Explore limits and take some risks. See what happens when you change the shape of your mouth, when you make a trill with your tongue, and when you talk through it. See if you can make it sound sweet, or angry, or tough. Stand in your bathroom and pretend you're already a great player, a star, and wail away. Use your tongue to make "chucka-chucka" sounds. Try doing that on the inhale as well as the exhale. Have some faith in yourself. If you're still reading this book you must be an interesting person, and I guarantee you can make music.

So go for it. You don't need
anyone's permission. You can **play.**

HOW THE HARMONICA
CAN MAKE YOU BE MORE PLAYFUL
(WHICH IS THE WHOLE POINT OF THIS BOOK)

▓ ▓ ▓ ▓ ▓ ▓ ▓ ▓ ▓ ▓

⋯⟩ **WHILE YOU'RE PLAYING HARMONICA YOU CAN'T YELL AT YOUR KIDS OR YOUR DOG, AND YOU CAN'T FROWN.**

FURTHERMORE, THE HARMONICA:

- Is a self-contained pomposity-reducing unit.
- Keeps you from thinking too much about all the world's bad news.
- Makes babies happy, which makes you happy.
- Makes dogs sing along.
- Makes you feel more like a cowboy or blues singer, or both.
- Goes with any outfit, including chaps and a ten-gallon hat or dark sunglasses, or all three—not to mention your evening gown. And (extra bonus) it will fit in the teensiest evening purse, too!
- Is a handy tool in your pocket (or are you just glad to see me?).
- Can make train sounds.
- Can say "ma-ma."
- Is modestly priced, so you have money left over to buy an ice cream cone.
- Will not allow anyone (including yourself) to take you too seriously.

CHAPTER 2

⌒⌒

Breathing

and
Other Essentials...

"Breathing is good for you."
— HIPPOCRATES

ONE DAY I WAS GIVING MY TEENAGE SON Daniel a driving lesson. I've never thought of myself as a control freak, but it was amazing how uncomfortable I felt when the steering wheel was in Daniel's hands. He drove too slow; he drove too fast. He seemed too nervous; he seemed too relaxed. I wasn't sure he saw that woman pushing a stroller stepping off the curb (he had, but I wasn't sure). He rolled slowly through a stop sign, something I had gotten a ticket for only months earlier.

I was a wreck. It wasn't that Daniel was a bad driver; for someone just learning to drive he was doing fine. It was that I was a bad teacher. I found myself snapping at my son. I seemed to be short of breath, and when I got out of the car I actually felt dizzy.

Later that week I attended a beginning yoga class at my local YMCA. The instructor kept reminding us to breathe long, slow breaths all the way from our belly. It felt great. I was calm and at peace with the world.

The next time I went out driving with Daniel I found myself starting to get anxious all over again, even though his driving was coming along fine. Then I remembered breathing in the yoga class, and it hit me that there in the car with Dan I wasn't breathing at all. No wonder I was dizzy, anxious, and grumpy. I concentrated on breathing slowly in and out, while Daniel drove into a tree. Later, in the hospital, I was still breathing . . .

No, just kidding. Daniel was making fine progress, and so was I, as his teacher, as long as I remembered to breathe.

Sometimes we play with our breathing just for fun. Have you ever played the game where you hold your breath while passing a graveyard? I think this has something to do with not letting bad spirits steal your soul. Or maybe it's just a way to make kids be quiet for a little while on road trips. At any rate, it is a game we play with our breath.

Breathing also comes in handy when you are playing the harmonica. The harmonica is unusual in that some of the time you are breathing air *in* while you are playing. We are accustomed to breathing out slowly, as we do when we speak or sing, but generally when we need to get air we breathe it in quickly. With the harmonica you will need to breathe out *and* in, sometimes slowly, sometimes switching back and forth fairly quickly between the two. All this breathing is really good for you, and I would suggest you just go ahead and do a lot of it. There's no wrong way to have fun blowing in and out of a harmonica. See if you can make it sound like the end of a great symphony, or pretend you are Bob Dylan trying to figure out a new song.

On October 19, 2006, a headline on the front page of the *Wall Street Journal* stated, "One More Reason to Play the Harmonica: It's Good for the Pipes." Imagine the sound of thousands of stockbrokers playing "We're in the Money" as they are driven to work, and "Brother, Can You Spare a Dime?" as they walk home.

HARMONICA *lesson* #7

···⟩ **REMEMBERING TO BREATHE,** relax your lips and gently blow and draw through holes 1, 2, and 3. Do it slowly, then fast like a choo-choo train:

123 123 123 123 123 123 123

↑   ↓   ↑   ↓   ↑   ↓   ↑

Think of it like a vacuum cleaner: when you want to focus the suction of the vacuum cleaner in a narrow area, you use the crevice tool, which is like a single note. When you want to vacuum a wider area, you use the wider floor brush, which is like playing several notes at once. If you breathe gently into a harmonica in this wider way, like you just did, it produces a chord—that is, three or more musical tones sounded at the same time. In the beginning, making a chord on the harmonica will be easier for you than single notes. The most common chords are pleasing and harmonious. Gentle, even breath applied to all three (or four) notes will help you to get this sweet tone.

Vacuuming the floor the Regular Way:

1. Get out the vacuum cleaner.
2. Plug it in.
3. Vacuum the floor.

Vacuuming the floor the Playful Way:

1. Put on a tuxedo or evening gown.
2. Get out the vacuum cleaner.
3. Plug it in.
4. Bow or curtsy to the vacuum cleaner.
5. Pretend you are Fred Astaire or Ginger Rogers, and pretend your partner, the vacuum cleaner, is Fred Astaire or Ginger Rogers.
6. Dance around gracefully while vacuuming the floor.

Now let's explore what we can do with these chords on the low end of the harp. (The harmonica goes by a lot of nicknames: harp is one, from French harp or mouth harp; also, mouth organ, pocket piano, and band in your pocket. I call mine "Elwood.") Try playing very evenly and slowly. And (this is important) try playing quietly. See what you can do with only a little breath. You will find that it helps if you use your nose as a pressure valve—if you breathe in or out through your nose while you breathe in and out through the harmonica, you'll find that you can lessen the airflow when necessary to make sweeter tones on your harmonica, not to mention your vacuum cleaner. This is because it really takes very little air to play the harmonica, and many (though not all) beginners blow too hard when they play. Use your nose to eliminate excess air from your lungs or to breathe in the air you need even as you keep playing.

HARMONICA *lesson* #8

⤵ **PLAY THE CHORDS CHARTED OUT BELOW,** slowly at first, and then faster. Remember to play with a nice, wide mouth, since you are playing chords, so that all three notes get an equal amount of air. Also, tilt the harmonica at a slight angle so that the part away from your mouth is a little higher than the part in your mouth. **Think of the down arrow as pointing at you, and the up arrow as pointing away—that's the direction you should play.** Play for as long as you like, varying your tempo for fun. End on a long draw, like a train coming to a stop. Don't try to figure out what song it is—it isn't. Think of it more like the sound of a train in your dreams:

123 123 123 123 123 123 123 123 123 123
↓   ↓   ↑   ↑   ↓   ↓   ↑   ↑   ↓   ↓   etc.

Now try playing long chords very gently, holding each inhale and exhale for a steady count of four:

123   123   123
↓   ↑   ↓

Now try that again, only tap your tongue ever so lightly against the roof of your mouth like you're saying "hu-tuh," so that each long inhale or exhale is broken into two even parts. **Now put on a chicken suit and do it again while vacuuming the floor.** Don't focus on incorrect or correct here; **you're exploring your inner chicken.** Just try to make it pleasing to yourself—nobody but yourself—and be patient. Remember, on the harmonica, whether or not you're wearing a chicken outfit, you're a kid again. There's no schedule and no agenda, and there won't ever be any tests.

HARMONICA *lesson* #9

⋯⟫ **I KNOW THE REASON YOU DECIDED TO PLAY THE HARMONICA** was so you could play Beethoven's greatest work, "Mary Had a Little Lamb," and now's your chance. Remember, open your mouth wide enough to cover three holes. Now rest the harp inside your mouth on your lower lip, tilting it so the holes are pointing slightly down into your mouth, with your upper lip halfway over the top cover. Now gently whistle into the middle hole. Try to maintain a single note, but don't get too hung up on it at this stage—it will come with time. Let's play the song:

⋯⟫ MARY HAD A LITTLE LAMB

5	4	4	4	5	5	5
↑	↓	↑	↓	↑	↑	↑

4	4	4	5	6	6
↓	↓	↓	↑	↑	↑

5	4	4	4	5	5	5
↑	↓	↑	↓	↑	↑	↑

5	4	4	5	4	4
↑	↓	↓	↑	↓	↑

Back when I first started playing, I walked up and down the road inhaling and exhaling through the harmonica for hours on end. I learned that places with an echo—stairwells, bathrooms, parking garages, state penitentiaries—were great for hearing what I was doing, because the music bounced back to me like I was in a great hall or canyon. My playing sounded better in those places, fuller and one step removed like it was already a memory or a recording. In time I also learned that playing gently was a good thing—the reeds in the harmonica seemed to enjoy soft treatment, and it took no more than the breath to blow a feather off my hand to make a pretty tone, especially if I opened up and played from my belly.

I won't lie to you—I had barely begun playing before my imagination took over and I saw myself on stage, caressed by the warm rays of a spotlight, making beautiful music before a rapt audience. A girl I had a crush on was there watching me, as well as the members of my extended family and all the teachers and students from my school. After the show I signed autographs before being whisked away in my limousine with the girl and a couple of her friends.

Or maybe I was a hobo, like one of those penniless travelers who sometimes found their way to my hometown. Walking through the woods looking for a place to sleep, I was a free man. I curled up with my belongings on a pile of dry leaves, pulled my harp out of my inside coat pocket, and played to the trees and stars, who told me to shut up and go to sleep.

Even then I knew I should have spent my time getting good grades so I could go to the best possible school and get a high-paying job, rather than romanticizing poverty or fantasizing about being a star. Certainly that's what I tell my son Daniel, who is obsessed with playing the bouzouki and wants to buy an electric bass banjo. Luckily, there is no learner's permit or license required for playing these instruments. But I should understand what Daniel is seeking; the sounds I discovered on the harmonica became the music of my life,

HARMONICA *lesson* #10

···⟩ **"OH! SUSANNA" WAS THE FIRST SONG I EVER LEARNED IN FULL,** with the help of a small sheet that came with the harmonica. Remember to tilt the harmonica so the side away from you is a little higher than the side in your mouth. Also, once you get a single note, try to keep the harmonica in your mouth as much as possible. In other words, don't keep taking it out and putting it in again while you're playing the song, because then you have to reshape your mouth with each note, which is inefficient. One other note: I've tried to pick familiar, simple songs in this book to help you learn, but if you don't know one, go give a listen. Music is a language, and part of how you learn is by listening.

4	4	5	6	6	6	6	5	4
↑	↓	↑	↑	↑	↓	↑	↑	↑

4	5	5	4	4	4
↓	↑	↑	↓	↑	↓

4	4	5	6	6	6	6	5	4
↑	↓	↑	↑	↑	↓	↑	↑	↑

4	5	5	4	4	4
↓	↑	↑	↓	↓	↑

5	5	6	6	6	6	6	5	4	4
↓	↓	↓	↓	↓	↑	↑	↑	↑	↓

···⟩

HARMONICA *lesson* #10

4	4	5	6	6	6	6	5	4
↑	↓	↑	↑	↑	↓	↑	↑	↑

4	5	5	4	4	4
↓	↑	↑	↓	↓	↑

"OH! SUSANNA"

along with what I heard sung around our family fireplace, the roar of cars speeding down the interstate highway at night, subways rushing under the streets of Manhattan, thunderstorms, crashing waves, the whistle of wind over the Great Plains, trains in the distance or planes overhead, and blessed silence—all interwoven with the sound of my harmonica, both what I already could play and what I imagined myself playing, someday.

We need breath to live, and we need breath to play the harmonica. The harmonica is life. No, wait, that's ridiculous. But it is fair to say that breathing is important in both life and playing the harmonica. So remember to breathe, learn to get some control over it, and you'll be a better person—or at least a healthier person.

As I said earlier, the harmonica is unusual in that you make music by breathing *in* as well as *out*. We all know how to breathe out slowly (we do this whenever we talk), but I don't know of many situations where we breathe in slowly. Practicing yoga, scuba diving, and smoking marijuana come to mind, though I have not done the second two of these things myself—or at least I have never inhaled.

How to breathe the Regular Way:

1. Get born.
2. Doctor slaps your behind.
3. Breathing goes on autopilot.

How to breathe the Playful Way:

1. Breathe like a dog: get on all fours and pant (but it is bad manners to sniff someone's butt or stick your nose in his crotch).
2. Try breathing like a hummingbird (1,000 breaths per second).
3. Breathe like Darth Vader.
4. Go up to a mountaintop or to a nice park and breathe the fresh air. Make breathing more fun by filling the air around with nice smells—flowers, fresh-baked cookies, a wet dog.

In this chapter you've learned a little about breathing, you've started playing music, and you may have also done some vacuuming. Feel free to go over these songs as often as you need, because they will help you learn. If you feel inspired, pick out some other songs by ear or make up one of your own. You're part of a great tradition, and you are on your way to making your own music.

CHAPTER 3

LISTENING

Big Ears are Pretty

"I would rather have Dumbo's ears than my nose."
—PINOCCHIO

ONCE I WAS IN A BAND THAT WAS ASSEMBLED TO PLAY for a New Year's Eve party. The bass player was a fellow named Mike Shea. Mike knew I was looking for a new job. There was another member of the band, a trumpet player named Steve Hanselman, who had just been promoted to publisher of a division of a large publishing house. One rehearsal during a break Mike said to me, "Hey, Sam, you're interested in books and publishing, right?" I said I was, and he said I should get to know Steve the trumpet player. I said that sounded fine, but I didn't understand why it was so important to Mike and forgot all about it.

Next week Mike said, "So, Sam, have you talked to Steve yet?" I said no, but that he seemed like a nice guy. "He's a wheel in publishing, Sam. You really should talk to him." I said I would and promptly forgot all about it. Finally, the third week Mike said, "So Sam, you're into writing and books, and you're looking for a new job, right?" And I said, "Uh, sure," not really clear why Mike kept bringing this up at a rehearsal.

"And Steve's a wheel in publishing."

"Uh huh," I answered, still not understanding what Mike was getting at. "So you should talk to him about getting a job!" Mike said, dragging me over to Steve.

So, I met Steve and I got a new job. All that time I was hearing Mike's words, but I wasn't really listening to him. Fortunately for me, Mike was doing my listening for me. But it's best if we learn to pay attention for ourselves.

Among musicians it is a compliment to be told you have "big ears."

Having big ears means you know how to listen, which is fundamental to playing well. Or maybe you just have really big ears. Anyhow, using our ears is essential to enjoying music, learning to play, improvising, and just about everything else musical.

Listening is essential to more than music. Has there ever been a time when you were so absolutely sure you were right, and then something happened that made you really listen to the person you were arguing with, see things differently, and even change your mind? Or have you ever assumed you knew what was going on, like me in the last story, when in fact you were missing the entire point?

Understanding what we are hearing is a tricky thing, but if we don't learn how to listen we'll spend a good deal of our time confused and a step behind. If we learn to listen we'll be better prepared for the next moment, the next week, and the rest of our lives, which is a good reason for all of us to hone our listening skills. And also, something good might come our way.

Try this: turn off any radios, computers, televisions, and recordings, shut your eyes, and for five minutes pay attention to everything you hear. Isolate the different sounds. Is this one far away? Is that one nearby? Are the sounds to the left or the right of you? Is there a steady, repeating sound? Is there another sound that you only heard once? Is that pounding on your door important? Those fire alarms? The sirens coming closer and closer? Why is that man shouting through a megaphone? And what is that smell? Relax and enjoy the sounds of the world around you, listening and absorbing everything.

Now that you're in a Red Cross shelter, listen to some music with your eyes closed. Let go of your preconceptions and try to hear the music just as it is, without judging or filtering the sound. How does the song begin? Is there an introduction? Do you notice a repeated theme or musical idea? See if you can isolate one instrument from another. Pay close attention to the rhythms of each part: the beat of the drum, the steady strum of a guitar, the voice of the singer, the bass, the piano, and so on. The heartbeat of music is rhythm, and every part of what you are hearing is driven by rhythm. Pay attention to how the music moves, getting louder and softer, changing the beat, with some instruments dropping in and others out. Notice that even silence can be a part of making music.

Listen to as much music as you can. Pay special attention to the harmonicas you hear out there, whether in a great old blues song or in an advertising jingle piped through the sound system at the grocery store. I think you'll be surprised at how often you'll hear the harmonica, if you pay attention. Sometimes focusing on a detail like this can give us a little vacation from the worries of life. It's not that our problems will go away, but taking a break from dwelling on them allows us to recharge our creative energy and gain perspective.

When you're playing in a band, it's *really* important to listen. I was once playing in a loud rock band in a bar. When it came time for me to solo, I grabbed my harp and started wailing into the microphone. I couldn't really hear what I was doing, but I was feeling good. Unfortunately, about a verse into my solo, I realized I was wailing in the wrong key! It sounded horrible and I was terribly embarrassed. It's good to listen, and it's good to be able to hear.

Another thing you should do is check out a variety of harmonica players. These are some amazing musicians, and each player has his or her own tone, just as every student I've ever taught has his or her unique sound.

WHAT FOLLOWS IS
A BY-NO-MEANS-COMPREHENSIVE
LIST OF *famous players* WHO DEMONSTRATE
A VARIETY OF STYLES.

For blues:

Little Walter, Sonny Boy Williamson I, Sonny Boy Williamson II, Sonny Terry, James Cotton, Big Walter Horton, Big Mama Thornton, Paul Butterfield, Junior Wells, Jimmy Reed, Charlie Musselwhite, John Mayall, Annie Raines, Mark Ford

BESTSELLING
HARMONICA RECORDS *of* ALL TIME

············> **IT'S NOT "WHITE CHRIST-MAS," NOR "SOMETHING" BY THE BEATLES,** or even by Mariah Carey. The truth is that a harmonica record is not going to compete with the big records of all time—but then, since Benny Goodman hung up his cleats, neither has a clarinet record hit that level, and it's been a while since we've had a saxophone hit like "Yakety Sax" or a standard that featured a drum solo like "Wipeout." Fact is, best-selling records are more about showbiz than music.

As for the harmonica—for many years it wasn't even considered a legitimate instrument, but that changed with the all-harmonica group the Harmonicats' recording of "Peg O' My Heart," which was a best-selling record of 1947 that went on to become one of the best-selling singles ever. Ironically, the Harmonicats were aided by a musician strike, which resulted in "Peg O' My Heart" getting an unusual amount of airplay. Because the musician's union didn't consider harmonica players legitimate musicians, the record was one of the few that could be played on the radio during the strike. The success of this record helped convince the musicians' union to reclassify the harmonica as a legitimate instrument.

But in general, there are few harmonica hits. Rather, the harmonica plays a role in hits, like any other instrument. In 1937, John Lee Williamson (Sonny Boy Williamson I) had a hit in the segregated world called "race records" with "Good Morning, School Girl." Little Walter's "Juke" was a number-one hit

············>

BESTSELLING
HARMONICA RECORDS *of* ALL TIME
(continued)

on the R&B charts in 1952. Other hits that feature the harmonica include Stevie Wonder's "For Once in My Life," the Beatles' "Love Me Do," Paul Butterfield's "Born in Chicago," Bob Dylan's "Shelter from the Storm," Neil Young's "Heart of Gold," and Blues Traveler's "Run-around."

This short, incomplete list is intended to show the diversity of hit songs that have featured the harmonica. If you open your ears, you'll start hearing the harmonica everywhere, from truck commercials, where it is intended to convey manly western values, to avant-garde music, where it is used for its eerie, ghostly quality. **THE HARMONICA IS A HIT AND IT IS HERE TO STAY.**

For country or bluegrass:
Charlie McCoy, Mickey Raphael, Jimmy Fadden, Delbert McClinton

For rock, folk rock, and pop:
Stevie Wonder, Bruce Springsteen, Mick Jagger, Bob Dylan, Neil Young, John Sebastian Jr., Lee Oskar, Vicki Simpson, John Popper

For hip-hop:
Outkast, Yuri Lane

For jazz:
Toots Thielemans, Gregoire Maret, Howard Levy

For standards:
The Harmonicats, Tommy Morgan, the Harmonica Rascals

For classical:
Larry Adler, John Sebastian Sr., Tommy Reilly

Knowledge, opportunity, and the riches of memory and wisdom come from listening, which means we can't always be making noise, and this includes the chatter of our own minds. When we are in a conversation we may hear the other person's words, but if we are thinking about what we are going to say next we miss most of what the other person is saying. That's not listening. There are a lot of reasons why we fail to listen. When we are full of ourselves we don't listen well. When we are anxious we don't listen well. When we are fighting we don't listen well. Turn off the television and the computer and pay attention to the people and pets that are right there with you. If your dog is reciting the Gettysburg Address, perhaps it's time you listened to your therapist and tried some of those wonderful new medications.

When you play, listen without prejudice to the sounds that come out of your harmonica. Don't put yourself down. The beauty is there for you to create if you'll just allow it to happen. Have big ears when you are listening to other people's music. For instance, if a country song comes on, avoid knee-jerk reactions like cranking up the volume and shouting "Yee-haw!" at the top of your lungs and line dancing, or, conversely, saying "I hate country music" and turning it off. Give every kind of music a fair and intelligent chance. Don't just hear it—listen to it.

Make a practice of paying attention. Relax your body. Try to avoid distractions and fidgeting. Bring your whole heart and mind to the act of listening. Knowing when to be silent is a powerful tool of communication. Silence allows you to be aware. Give yourself permission to be silent and listen, and your imagination will blossom.

Learn to listen the Regular Way:

1. Sit on a chair.
2. Close your mouth (and no gum).
3. Fold your hands in your lap.
4. Stop fidgeting.
5. Place both feet on the ground.

Learn to listen the Playful Way:

1. Let your pre-teen or teenage children put on their favorite music, or if you are a teen, have your parents put on their favorite music.
2. Refrain from making smart-alecky comments.
3. Try to identify and follow different instruments, and give yourself extra points for following the bass or tuba line.
4. Go out and listen to a live music act you've never heard of before.

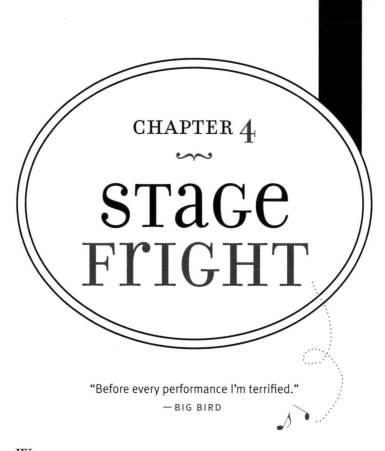

CHAPTER 4

STAGE FRIGHT

"Before every performance I'm terrified."
— BIG BIRD

WHEN I WAS A KID AND THEY WERE CHOOSING TEAMS I wasn't the last picked; I was the second-to-last picked. Yet in spite of my lack of talent and skill as an athlete, I loved to play, and I often imagined myself as a star. This daydream version of me did not blend well with the reality of playing team sports, where I was very ordinary and sometimes even embarrassingly bad. Let's just say I wasn't someone who helped lead my team to victory.

Like most of us, I was afraid of being laughed at for not being good enough. Fear itself became the problem, and ultimately it pushed me away from organized sports, even though I probably would have gone on to be the greatest professional basketball player of all time. (Instead, Michael Jordan got this honor. I could have kicked his ass. But that's not important now.)

We shouldn't allow fear to rule our lives, but all too often it does. Dave, a student of mine, was an investment banker. He was an accomplished man who didn't appear to lack confidence. At the first lesson Dave said he believed himself to be "without musical talent," but I hear this from many students and am usually able to persuade them to dismiss this negative self-image and to stop comparing themselves to Michael Jordan. Dave and I proceeded full steam ahead. Months later, when Dave had started to make great progress, he revealed to me that a primary reason for taking the lessons was to help him get over his terror of speaking or performing in front of people. I was as impressed watching Dave's progress as I was at hearing Sonny Terry or Paul Butterfield perform their magic; his personal victory meant as much as another's public accomplishment. Dave's big moment came when he performed in front of friends and family at his grandmother's birthday party.

Humans are hardwired to feel fear in stressful situations; it's a survival tactic. For many of us nothing is more stressful than having to perform in front of others. Our bodies react to these situations as though we were running from a pack of wolves. Pounding heart, dry mouth, shaky knees—we've all been there. This is stage fright. Stage fright is quite normal. After all, getting up and doing something in front of others doesn't come naturally, so it is not surprising that we have some kind of physiological, mental, and emotional reaction. Stage fright is a combination of nervousness, excitement, and anticipation that also infuses us with the energy and alertness we need to perform. The trick is to not let it overwhelm us. You've heard of the idea of picturing your audience in their underwear. I would suggest picturing your audience with underwear on their heads.

Take the harmonica and hold it in your hand—it's a beautiful machine, small, yet capable of making magic. Gently play this simple and, I hope, familiar song—the melody to "Michael, Row the Boat Ashore." Keep the harmonica in your mouth for as long as you can— if possible, through the whole song. This makes the music smoother. Try to play single notes—think *whistle*—but don't worry if you're not there yet.

4	5	6	5	6	6	6	5	6	6	6
↑	↑	↑	↑	↑	↓	↑	↑	↑	↓	↑
Mi-	chael	row	the	boat	a-	shore, hal-	le-	lu-		jah

5	6	6	5	5	5	4	4	4	5	4	4
↑	↑	↑	↑	↓	↑	↓	↑	↓	↑	↓	↑
Mi-	chael	row	the	boat	a-	shore, hal-	le-	lu-	u-	jah

Does it sound like the song as you play? Do you feel like you are at summer camp? Is it beginning to be music? I hope so. More importantly, was it fun? It can be fun even if you're only just starting to get the hang of a new thing.

If there was a dog nearby, did it start barking? Many dogs like to bark along with harmonicas. They are singing along. Once I had a dog that would happily lean his head back and howl like a wolf when I played. It happens that this dog was a ninety-pound collie-shepherd mix, so nobody argued with him when he started to howl. Later on he started to play the harmonica and became the front man, or dog, for a Chicago blues band. Sometimes cats get in on the action, too. Almost everybody likes music.

But maybe, very possibly you didn't have a good experience. Perhaps you thought your playing was mediocre (that most dispiriting of words) or just plain bad. If that's the case, remember this—at least the dog's having a good time. If your playing doesn't sound as good as you'd like early on, maybe you just need to change your attitude. If you can't do something well, then enjoy doing it badly!

Overcome stage fright the Regular Way:

1. Practice a lot.
2. Read books.
3. Join Toastmasters.
4. Take beta blockers.
5. Go to a hypnotist or therapist for treatment.

Overcome stage fright the Playful Way:

1. Join an amateur choir, chorus, or barbershop quartet.
2. Go to a Karaoke bar.
3. Imagine everyone in the audience wearing stupid-looking boxer shorts (them—not you).
4. Put on a costume and sing in front of the mirror or to your dog.
5. Imagine your shrink singing in really stupid-looking boxer shorts to your dog.

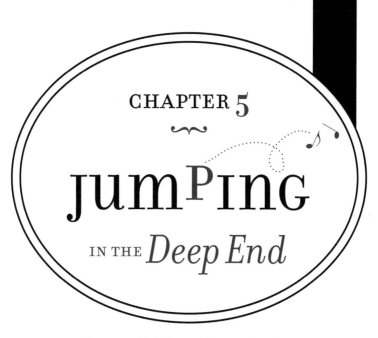

CHAPTER 5

JUMPING

IN THE *Deep End*

"My mom said she learned how to swim when someone took her out in the lake and threw her off the boat. I said, 'Mom, they weren't trying to teach you how to swim.'"
— PAULA POUNDSTONE

WHEN I WAS SEVEN YEARS OLD I SPENT A SUMMER AT an away camp called Sharparoon with my older sister and two older brothers. That summer I arrived at Sharparoon afraid of sleeping in the dark, prone to bedwetting, and unable to swim. People had tried to teach me to swim, but I had never, quite literally, taken the plunge. I was ashamed of my shortcomings, as I saw them. I think adults often don't realize how aware children are of their personal difficulties and how embarrassing these difficulties can be. I was way harder on myself than anyone else was. I saw myself as a wimp. I *was* a wimp. And so I arrived at camp that summer determined to improve myself, though at the time I never articulated these goals to anyone, least of all myself, since I had never read a self-help book.

My siblings kept an eye out for me that summer, but they were busy and I had a lot of time to myself. I befriended a fellow camper named Kevin. Kevin and I walked around Sharparoon like we owned it, comparing our hometowns, bragging about our families, and exaggerating our past exploits, which couldn't have been many, considering we were seven years old. But when Kevin would suggest that we go for a swim in the lake, as he did several times daily, I had to beg off.

Sharparoon was mostly populated by kids from Harlem and the Bronx in New York City, and some of them seemed pretty tough, but one thing many of them couldn't do was swim. So here was another incentive for me to learn to swim—I could impress my fellow campers.

One day we were at the lake and the counselors were determining what level swimmers we all were. Beginners and intermediate swimmers had to swim inside the dock. Advanced swimmers could swim outside the dock and could attempt the swim across the lake. I volunteered to test at the advanced level.

I remember standing there, looking down into the murky green-brown water of that upstate New York lake, but I'm not sure what I was thinking. If my siblings had seen me they would have certainly put a stop to it, since I didn't even qualify as an intermediate swimmer.

Then I jumped in.

It was the first time I had ever been in water over my head, so I was quite startled as I sank down into the dark and the water changed from warm to cold around my legs and feet. I knew enough to hold my breath and could see the small circle of light above me. That was when my survival instinct kicked in. I struggled frantically to the surface and began treading water.

The first thing I saw was the recreation counselor and her assistant looking down at me with alarmed expressions on their faces. It was clear I was about to get the hook. I summoned up enough bravado to give the impression that I was confident to go on, although the counselor seemed doubtful. To pass the test I had to tread water for two minutes, float for a minute, and swim four laps. I accomplished the first two well enough and then began dog-paddling my way the length of the dock. On the second lap I heard an encouraging voice.

"Go, Sam, you're nearly there!" It was Kevin, running—well, walking the length of the dock, urging me on to success. And I did succeed, in a feat that may not amount to much in the world of athletics, but was for me one of my finest moments. Also, maybe a little stupid. But I was proud of myself, and from then on I was a swimmer.

I learned I could be brave that day. I also learned that I could try something new, something I thought I couldn't do—and succeed at doing it.

So I guess you see where I'm going with this story. It's time for you to get over your fear and learn how to skydive.

Perhaps you're thinking, "I'm not a child learning to swim, I'm a grownup with a busy life. I'm not afraid of the harmonica; I'm just not good at it. I'm not creative. I'm too old. I'm too busy. I have attention deficit disorder. I'm right-handed. I don't have enough soul. Besides, playing music won't make me any money or help me meet influential people."

Behind this sort of thinking is a message that got into our system long ago that says, "I can't do this, and I'm going to look like an idiot trying, so I won't try." This fear haunts many of us. There are related voices, outside and inside our heads, telling us to have another donut. And every morning I hear a voice that says, "Ten more minutes, you can sleep ten more minutes." But my point is this—we have to ignore the naysayers and our internal negativity and just go for it. There is an even shorter way to say this, but Nike has trademarked the phrase.

This is where the harmonica comes in. No one is telling you to play the harmonica, so there is no outside pressure. The harmonica is not found on your typical school curriculum. It is not the instrument that parents generally urge kids to play. It isn't even an instrument that your fellow musicians ask you to learn. It isn't fashionable, and it doesn't go on your résumé or your application to an Ivy League school. It won't make you rich or get you the guy or girl.

So why choose the harmonica? I'll tell you why my students do. Some think they can't play anything else and turn to the harmonica

---> GREAT MOMENTS *in* HARMONICA HISTORY

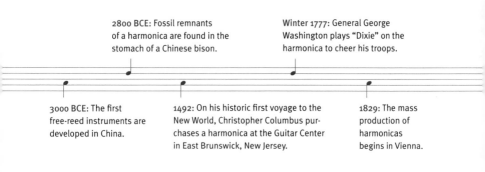

2800 BCE: Fossil remnants of a harmonica are found in the stomach of a Chinese bison.

Winter 1777: General George Washington plays "Dixie" on the harmonica to cheer his troops.

3000 BCE: The first free-reed instruments are developed in China.

1492: On his historic first voyage to the New World, Christopher Columbus purchases a harmonica at the Guitar Center in East Brunswick, New Jersey.

1829: The mass production of harmonicas begins in Vienna.

because they believe it's easy to learn. And it's true; the harmonica is an instrument that allows you to get somewhere almost immediately, though mastery is another matter. Another reason people want to play the harmonica is its accessibility—it is an inexpensive, tiny instrument that you can bring with you almost anywhere. The harmonica was the first instrument played in outer space, by astronaut Wally Schirra on the *Gemini VI* spacecraft in 1965.

The primary attraction of the harmonica for me is its folksy beauty. From the moment we first play the harmonica we can make it cry, or mourn, or laugh, or shout, or whisper. It is an instrument of the people. It has soul without pretension. It is something we can do ourselves when we need to take a little time out from the world.

Most of us constantly compare ourselves to other people. Taught to rank the world in terms of winners and losers, we live in fear of being left out or looking foolish, and we learn to pay close attention to who's in and who's out. We apply these standards in our families, in our friendships, at school, and at work. We even rank our philosophy

1830: Threatened by Vienna's stockpile of harmonicas, Paris responds by mass producing accordions.

1857: Mattias Hohner begins manufacturing harmonicas in his kitchen.

1863: Confederate soldier Elmer Fluderbuck's life is saved when a bullet aimed for his heart is deflected by his Hohner harmonica, which he purchased in East Brunswick, New Jersey.

October 31, 1852: An assassination attempt on President Millard Fillmore is foiled when the bullet is deflected by a harmonica in his breast pocket.

1862: Hohner begins exporting harmonicas to East Brunswick, New Jersey.

HARMONICA *lesson* #11

⋯⟩ **LET'S GIVE THE OLD SONG "YOU ARE MY SUNSHINE" A TRY.** Try shaping the inside of your mouth like you are whistling as you play to get a single note, breathing gently as you go. If you are still getting more than one note, try to make the melody note the higher note—the note to the right side of your mouth—so the melody stands out a little more. Remember not to criticize yourself as you play—just jump in and do it.

3	4	4	5	5	5	4	5	4	4
↑	↑	↓	↑	↑	↑	↓	↑	↑	↑
You	are	my	sun-	shine,	my	only		sun-	shine

4	4	5	5	6	6	6	5	5
↑	↓	↑	↓	↓	↓	↑	↓	↑
You	make	me	hap-	py	when	skies	are	grey	⋯⟩

⋯⟩ GREAT MOMENTS *in* HARMONICA HISTORY

1908: Henry Ford begins mass-marketing the harmonica in one color: black.

1920: The sale and manufacture of harmonicas is outlawed in the United States. The ban leads to a mushrooming of illegal harmonica playing, and the rise of Al Capone in East Brunswick, New Jersey.

1864: Thousands of Civil War soldiers die after rushing heedlessly into battle, thinking that they are protected by the harmonicas in their pockets.

October 30, 1938: Orson Welles repeatedly interrupts a Mercury Theatre radio with a rendition of "Oh! Susanna" on the harmonica, terrifying millions.

and religion, claiming this one to be preeminent, that one the most virtuous, the most generous, the deepest, wisest, or most esoteric. We compare everything to everything, everyone to everyone.

For someone learning to make music, comparisons can be

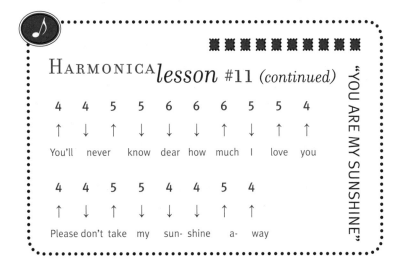

HARMONICA *lesson* #11 *(continued)*

"YOU ARE MY SUNSHINE"

4	4	5	5	6	6	6	5	5	4
↑	↓	↑	↓	↓	↓	↑	↓	↑	↑
You'll	never	know	dear	how	much	I	love	you	

4	4	5	5	4	4	5	4
↑	↓	↑	↓	↓	↓	↑	↑
Please	don't	take	my	sun-	shine	a-	way

December 16, 1965: Astronaut Wally Schirra plays "Jingle Bells" on the harmonica while in outer space.

1999: The *Wall Street Journal* recognizes Dr. Henry T. Bahnson, former chairman of surgery at the University of Pittsburgh, and Dr. James F. Antakion, professor of biomedical engineering and computer science at Carnegie Mellon University, for the work on the physics and physiology of playing the harmonica.

November 1973: A subpoenaed tape of President Richard M. Nixon playing the harmonica is cut short; there follows an 18½ minute gap in the recording.

1989: A super computer developed by the Massachusetts Institute of Technology plays cross harp with legendary bluesman B. B. King.

overwhelming. With the click of a button we can hear a recording of the greatest musicians in the world, which is wonderful but also crippling. When we compare ourselves to professional recordings, we are going head-to-head with the best versions of the most highly skilled musicians, as well as (in most cases) enhanced, remastered versions that even they couldn't reproduce live. Don't allow the extraordinary ability of a few and the slickness of expensive productions to defeat your healthy desire and right to play.

We should applaud those who are willing to risk being a fool. And what better way to risk this than by taking up the harmonica? Pick up your harmonica and make it sing and cry a little. Start out in a private place, breathing in and out. Make up your own song. Don't worry about any rules or what makes it a song or even music—just breathe gently. Treat it like your first kiss. Unless your first kiss sucked because both of your braces got locked together.

···⟩ GREAT MOMENTS *in* HARMONICA HISTORY

2003: The Finnish harmonica quartet Sväng is founded, forever changing our view of Finland.

2006: Britney Spears and Angelina Jolie both give birth to baby harmonicas. DNA testing reveals the identity of the father to be a man known as "Sonny Boy" from East Brunswick, New Jersey.

2005: Hollywood star Nicole Kidman divorces Tom Cruise when she discovers him in bed with a harmonica.

2007: A dancing baby elephant is videotaped playing the harmonica (see YouTube).

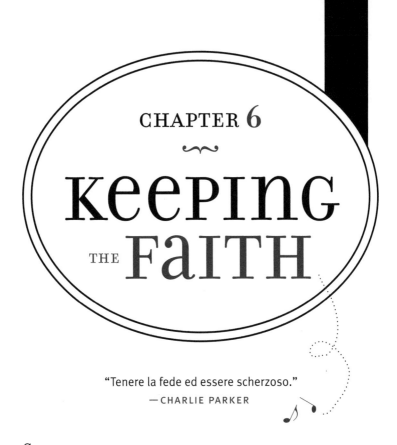

CHAPTER 6

KEEPING
THE FAITH

"Tenere la fede ed essere scherzoso."
—CHARLIE PARKER

SOME YEARS AGO MY FRIEND ERIC WENT TO ITALY ON an extended business trip. He enrolled in an intensive language program, which meant he spent four hours a day conjugating verbs and learning conversational Italian. After class he'd go to an outdoor café to do his homework and listen to the people around him. At first he couldn't understand a word, but he loved to let the sounds of this beautiful, exotic language wash over him. It seemed that everyone was talking passionately about love and art.

Several verb-conjugating weeks later, Eric sat at his usual table drinking his usual cappuccino and studying for a vocabulary test.

Gradually Eric became aware of an intense discussion between a man and a woman at the next table and realized that he understood every word. All his work had paid off! He shifted in his chair to hear what the couple was saying. One surreptitious glance revealed a tall, well-dressed man and a classic Italian beauty with long black hair. Eric imagined she worked as a curator at the museum across the piazza, and perhaps he worked at the consulate.

As he pieced together the overheard phrases, Eric realized that the conversation was about neither love nor art. Rather, it was about the man's habit of leaving his underwear on the floor, and the woman's unwillingness to screw the cap back on the toothpaste tube.

But the important thing was that Eric had made the leap to understanding a new language. Now he could argue in Italian with his girlfriend about putting the cap back on the toothpaste tube and doing the laundry. In fact, he had picked up a few choice words about that very subject. All he had to do was find a girlfriend who spoke Italian.

Learning how to play a musical instrument is like that. Not arguing in Italian, but the sudden understanding after a period of effort

HARMONICA *lesson* #12

---> **THE NOTES** on a ten-hole diatonic harmonica in the key of C are:

Hole:	1	2	3	4	5	6	7	8	9	10
Draw:	D	G	B	D	F	A	B	D	F	A
Blow:	C	E	G	C	E	G	C	E	G	C

and learning. It is a mystery how we do it, but if we keep plugging away, one day the pieces of the puzzle come together, and we discover we have made the leap to understanding a new language, whether it is music, Italian, or "romance."

Let's take another look at the harmonica. It is really quite an uncomplicated little thing—two sets of ten reeds, one for blow notes and one for draw notes, two plates to cover them, and ten holes to blow through. The harmonica is as simple as a pencil or a paintbrush. There we have it: nineteen notes (2 draw and 3 blow are the same note). It's really amazing how much music you can make with these few notes.

HARMONICA *lesson* #13

····} ONE WAY TO UNDERSTAND THE NOTES of any ten-hole diatonic harmonica, regardless of key, is in terms of the *do re mi fa so la ti* scale. That would look like this:

Hole:	1	2	3	4	5	6	7	8	9	10
Draw:	RE	SO	TI	RE	FA	LA	TI	RE	FA	LA
Blow:	DO	MI	SO	DO	MI	SO	DO	MI	SO	DO

When you change harmonicas—like, say, to the key of A—the harmonica is still arranged in this same do-re-mi order of notes, only now it is in the key of A. If you buy a D harmonica, it's that same arrangement, only in D. In other words, once you've learned to play a C harmonica (or whatever key you first own), you've learned to play all the ten-hole harmonicas, because the diatonic harmonic system is designed to change the key for you! You can also play it in Italian!

To celebrate, let's try playing "When the Saints Go Marching In," one of the grand songs in the American repertoire, and one for which I don't need to pay royalties. In the great city of New Orleans there is a tradition of street parades with a brass band leading funeral processions, with the band playing a hymn like "Just a Closer Walk with Thee" out to the cemetery, and a celebratory, danceable song like "Saints" on the way back.

HARMONICA *lesson* #14

···⟩ **LET'S START BY LEARNING THE FOLLOWING RIFF** (a riff is a short series of notes, especially one that is repeated in improvisation). At this point you're probably still working on getting a single note. Remember, this takes time, so be patient. When you do succeed in obtaining a clear single note, try to keep the harmonica in your mouth while moving to the next note so you can keep your mouth in the shape that successfully channeled the air into a single tone. Okay, let's play:

4	5	5	6
↑	↑	↓	↑
O	when	the	saints

That's not so hard, right? Now play the following musical phrase:

4	5	5	6	4	5	5	6
↑	↑	↓	↑	↑	↑	↓	↑
O	when	the	saints	go	marching		in

···⟩

HARMONICA *lesson* #14 *(continued)*

Notice that this phrase is really just the riff above played twice. **When we are learning something new, like playing the harmonica or building a cold fusion reactor, it helps to break down the task into bite-sized pieces.** Start by learning a couple of notes, or a riff. Then you need to string the notes together in a phrase, and then string the phrases together in a verse. Once you have a verse, you have a whole song, because all you have to do is repeat it a few times. And once you have a song, you have enough energy to power a small city!

4	5	5	6	4	5	5	6
↑	↑	↓	↑	↑	↑	↓	↑
O	when	the	saints	go	marching		in

4	5	5	6	5	4	5	4
↑	↑	↓	↑	↑	↑	↑	↓
O	when	the	saints	go	marching		in

5	4	4	4	5	6	6	6	5
↑	↓	↑	↑	↑	↑	↑	↑	↓
Lord	I	want	to	be	in	that	number	

5	5	6	5	4	4	4
↑	↓	↑	↑	↑	↓	↑
When	the	saints	go	marching		in

Playing "When the Saints Go Marching In" the Regular Way:

1. Pick up your harmonica.
2. Play the notes as written.

Playing "When the Saints Go Marching In" the Playful Way:

1. Put on Mardi Gras beads and some feathers or a top hat.
2. Enjoy a few sips of your favorite beverage.
3. Enlist the help of any small children or friends in the vicinity and arm them with noisemakers such as pots and pans.
4. Play the song and lead a parade around the house, perhaps around the neighborhood, or, if you're at work (in which case this could end up being your funeral), around the office.
5. Be imaginative—add some notes and make up a new arrangement.

Now let's try playing the hymn "Ode to Joy," the anthem of the European Union. The melody first gained prominence as the prelude to the last movement of Beethoven's Ninth Symphony, which is a good lesson in itself: good ideas are used and reused, and this process is ongoing. The wonderful thing about this is that any of us can dive in and build on the ever-growing body of human creativity. You can borrow from Beethoven, or Hank Williams, or Sonny Boy Williamson, or Toni Morrison, or Albert Einstein, knowing that they too were part of this borrowing process that stretches all the way back to our ancestors in the Neolithic era arguing about the dirty underwear on the floor and the cap on the toothpaste tube.

Is it beginning to sound like music? I hope so. It takes time to learn something new, so don't be hard on yourself. Give yourself a pat on the back, or on your butt if you are a football player. Reward yourself in some small way after each practice. Have an ice cream, or buy yourself a new car. And also remember to take on this new thing in manageable pieces, a little at a time every day. Soon you'll have a fleet of cars and thirty extra pounds on your hips.

If it isn't sounding quite as good as you'd hoped, don't be

HARMONICA *lesson* #15

···⟩ **IF YOU'VE NEVER HEARD "ODE TO JOY,"** find it and listen to it several times. You'll notice some notes are held longer than others—do your best, trust your ear, and follow your instincts. As you play this song, remember that you can use your tongue bouncing lightly off the roof of the mouth to separate the notes. Imagine that you are lightly saying "ta ta," without actually saying the words. Remember, you're playing to express joy, not to mention European unity, so make it count. Don't rush yourself. **Here's "Ode to Joy":**

5	5	5	6	6	5	5	4
↑	↑	↓	↑	↑	↓	↑	↓

4	4	4	5	5	4	4
↑	↑	↓	↑	↑	↓	↓

5	5	5	6	6	5	5	4
↑	↑	↓	↑	↑	↓	↑	↓

4	4	4	5	4	4	4
↑	↑	↓	↑	↓	↑	↑

···⟩

HARMONICA *lesson* #15 (*continued*)

"ODE TO JOY"

4	4	5	4	4	5	5	5	4
↓	↓	↑	↑	↓	↑	↓	↑	↑

4	5	5	5	4	4	4	3
↓	↑	↓	↑	↓	↑	↓	↑

5	5	5	6	6	5	5	4
↑	↑	↓	↑	↑	↓	↑	↓

4	4	4	5	4	4	4
↑	↑	↓	↑	↓	↑	↑

discouraged. Play softly, go slow, and give yourself a chance to learn. This may take playing the song over and over again for days and weeks, which doesn't mean you're a musical incompetent. Even accomplished musicians learn this way. What you hear in a performance is only possible after lots of rehearsal. Think of a baby babbling—a few years later they can speak a language. Really, it's quite amazing.

And so are you.

CHAPTER 7

⌒

JUST a WHITE BOY LOST

in the Blues

"Seven years of college, down the drain."
—JOHN BELUSHI

SOME YEARS AGO MY BROTHER DAVE WROTE A SONG called "The Tupperware Blues," which he played at the National Tupperware Convention for thousands of screaming Tupperware fanatics—uh, I mean salespeople. Dave asked me to teach his editor, *Washington Post* newspaper columnist Gene Weingarten, to play the blues riff made famous in Muddy Waters' "Mannish Boy (I'm a Man)."

Gene has all the natural musical talent of a waffle iron, but I was able to teach him this riff over the phone. They pulled off the show without a hitch. The crowd went wild—admittedly, the crowd was wild before they sang the song, too—but all the same, it was a fabulous success. Gene felt like a rock star. He was a rock star. It was a moment of triumph. Women were throwing underwear at him, some of it in handy Tupperware containers.

Tragically, like Marlene Dietrich and J. D. Salinger, Gene chose not to play the harmonica in public again for many years. (Actually, Marlene never was that much of a harmonica player.) Finally, Dave was able to coax Gene out of retirement and he stepped onstage with the all-author band the Rock Bottom Remainders. The band launched into a rendition of the now-classic "Tupperware Blues." To my complete amazement, Gene had not gotten one bit better at playing the song.

In the last chapter you learned that great blues classic, "Ode to Joy." Just kidding! That would be Beethoven's "I Got the Blues in My Ode." We all feel like playing the blues sometimes. Every day people go to work or school or care for their children while they are struggling with heartache, illness, financial woes, or lost toothpaste tube caps, pretending to the outside world that they are fine. Playing the blues allows you to express deeper emotions without blowing your cover. It's therapeutic and cathartic and has no calories.

There is no music more emotionally expressive than the blues, and nothing wails quite like the harmonica played blues style. In this chapter we'll get you started on the road to your "harp's desire": playing the blues on your harmonica.

Desire can be a little scary. It can get us in trouble, landing us in places we shouldn't be, places where we are out of our depth. It can feel like a ride at the amusement park where you find yourself asking, as you are strapped in, "Why did I want to get on this thing?" Then the teacups begin to spin madly around and everyone squeals with the tension of the moment.

But if we tap into desire in a healthy way, there is no telling where it will take us—maybe to Memphis and Chicago to hear the blues, or to New Orleans. Maybe desire will take us to new creative heights in our own living room, playing with friends we've yet to meet. Maybe desire will get us in trouble, or maybe it will lead us to our true love (and what's the difference, really?).

Desire is dangerous, but it's **powerful.**

❉ ❉ ❉ ❉ ❉ ❉ ❉ ❉ ❉ ❉

I've been playing the blues since I was a kid. Sometimes I ask myself what originally attracted me and so many others like me to a music formed in the African American experience in the South, given my consummate Yankee whiteness. Maybe it was romantic yearnings for something other than what and where I was. Maybe I just wanted to feel like I knew something about pain and toughness and women, when I didn't. (I still don't know about women.) Or maybe I just had a need to connect to this deep part of the American soul. Whatever it was, it stuck, and the music was in me.

The greatest and lasting attraction of well-played blues for me is its eerie, edgy beauty—the wail of pain, the growl of anger, the whispers of seduction, the hunger of lust, the mystery of hoodoo, the whoop of victory, the despair of loss. There's really nothing like the blues to express raw emotion, and if you love the music of America, you have to wrestle with the blues.

Straight harp is very useful, but because of its expressive limitations it is not as popular as cross harp, or second position. However, I urge you to put some effort into learning straight harp, even if

HARMONICA *lesson* #16

···⟩ **BEFORE WE TALK MORE ABOUT PLAYING THE BLUES** on the harmonica, I need to explain something about the difference between playing what many call straight (or first position) harmonica and cross harp (or second position) harmonica. Although most harmonicas are labeled in one key, such as C major, **it is possible to play any one harmonica in several keys by changing which notes you emphasize.** However, most of the harmonica you hear is in one of the two positions that I mentioned above. You've already played in first position, or straight harp, if you've tried playing the songs up to this point in the book, and there are some examples of cross harp in this chapter.

Playing straight harp is like going to the grocery store and following your usual path and buying your usual groceries. Playing cross harp is like starting on the opposite side of the store and looking for new items that you've never tried before.

Here's how it works: Your major diatonic harmonica is designed for playing simple folk music, and so the notes of the major scale—do re mi fa so la ti do—are laid out in a pattern designed to help you play those songs as you breathe in and out through the instrument. **Playing songs based on the major scale, with the holes 1, 4, 7, and 10 blow as your home base note, is called straight harp, or first position.** The original way of playing the ten-hole major diatonic harmonica, straight harp is well suited to simple melodies like "Oh! Susanna," folk music, and any other type of music that you can play, or at least fake, using the major scale.

In addition to scales like the major scale, which you play one note at a time, there are two easily played chords on the harmonica. If you blow on the bottom three or four holes of a C harp you are playing a C major chord, and when you draw on these same holes you are playing a G major chord. If you have an A harmonica, the (bottom three- or four-hole)

···⟩

HARMONICA*lesson* #16 *(continued)*

blow chord is A major and the draw chord is E major. In first position, playing the blow chord is your home base. When playing the harmonica this
way, the blow chord will usually be the chord the song starts and ends on,
as well as the chord most often played throughout your song. The other
chord played on the bottom three holes—the draw chord—is a very common second chord for harmonizing melodies you can play on the major
scale. So, although you have a very limited choice of chords, you have
two that can get you pretty far, especially in simpler music.

blues is your primary interest—it will improve your playing in general and will come in handy for playing along with many styles of
music. Sometimes it's good to do things the old-fashioned way.

Blues, rock, country, and jazz require a wider range of expres-
sion, which harmonica players discovered they could get by playing
their instrument in a different key (or technically, a different mode,
but let's not worry about such a fine distinction here). In cross harp
the draw chord becomes the home base chord, rather than the blow
chord as in straight harp. It's sort of like we're playing a game of
baseball, only we've switched the names of the bases—now we're
calling first base home, second base first, and so on. To start playing
blues harp, see Harmonica Lesson #17 on the following page.

Were you able to do that? Congratulations! You're playing a C harmonica in the key of G. You're playing cross harp, or second-position harp. Now you need a good agent! Understanding this fully may
take some time, but the important thing to know is that when you are

HARMONICA *lesson #17*

···⟩ **IN BLUES HARP YOUR SONG WILL USUALLY START AND END ON THE DRAW CHORD,** which will also be the most useful chord throughout the song. Try it—very gently breathe in through the harmonica on the bottom three holes. If it sounds a little sour, open your nose and let a little air come in that way. Start on the draw and then switch to the blow, then back to the draw. Keep it going like a slow train running, always emphasizing and ending on the draw. **Remember to relax and not overblow (or overdraw)** — play gently.

123   123   123   123   123   123   123   123   123   123   (END ON THE

↓   ↓   ↑   ↑   ↓   ↓   ↑   ↑   ↓   ↓   DRAW CHORD!)

playing cross harp you are playing the harmonica in a key other than that for which it was originally designed. At right is a chart to help you figure this out. The key on the left is the key the harmonica plays straight harp in (songs like "Oh! Susanna"); the chart on the right is the key in which that same harmonica plays cross harp style.

Playing the harmonica in the key on the right, in cross harp or second position, results in a generally more versatile, soulful style of playing often associated with the blues. The primary reason cross harp is a more expressive and fluid way of playing the harmonica has to do with the art of "bending" notes, which is a way in which we lower the pitch of the notes, something like a slide guitar or trombone. Bending certain notes helps make the harmonica sound like a voice wailing.

STRAIGHT HARP KEY	CROSS HARP KEY
G	D
Ab	Eb
A	E
Bb	F
B	F# (Gb)
C	G
Db	Ab
D	A
Eb	Bb
E	B
F	C
F#	C# (Db)

Don't be discouraged if you have already tried bending notes on the harmonica and were unable to get a good sound, or if you are mystified by this and the whole idea of cross harp. These skills do take time to master, but in my experience many people are able to play a little cross harp almost immediately.

Let's play the blues riff made famous in Muddy Waters' "Mannish Boy (I'm a Man)." If you don't know this song, find it and listen to it. This song is like early rap: the band plays the same riff (da DA da da DA) over and over and over and over and over again, while the singer kind of chants in between about what a sexy hot young thing he is. Make sure you're starting on 3 blow, and in one breath, without stopping, play the first three notes by sliding back and forth. On the fourth note, try popping your tongue off the roof of your mouth, like you are saying "tuh" or "kuh" backward, only don't say it.

3	4	3	3	3
↑	↑	↑	↙*	↑

*BEND THIS DRAW NOTE DOWN A HALF-STEP

As I said, this riff is played over and over and over and over and over again, with two beats in between each for singing or improvising. You'll notice there is an asterisk next to the fourth note of the riff, the three draw, and that the arrow is bent (↙). If you can, try and bend this note down (make it lower in pitch) by raising your tongue up where you make the "tuh" or "kuh" sound just as you start playing the note and draw a little more air through the reed (not too much). Can you whistle? If so, try whistling backward and lowering the pitch of your whistle. The way your tongue moves as you do this is a lot like the action that creates bending. Don't worry about doing this per-fectly right away. Sometimes it takes weeks to be able to bend. Don't let frustration get in your way—if you're struggling, take a break, have some fun, breathe deeply, take a walk down Beale Street, and come back to it later.

Note for readers who want to understand more about bending: Bending a note on the harmonica means changing the pitch of the note you are playing down to a lower pitch. For example, if you are playing one draw on a C harmonica, the note is a D. You can bend one draw down one half-step until it becomes a Db (D flat), the next note below D in our musical scale. Imagine you are singing "Old MacDonald Had a Farm." When you come to the part "ee-i-ee-i-o!" the shape of your mouth and placement of your tongue when you shift from "e" to "o" is like what you do when you go from unbent one draw to bent one draw. If you're alone, just sing "e" and then a slightly lower pitched "o" out loud. Now do this in the harmonica, but breathing in and without using your vocal chords. Also, tilt the part of the harmonica that's not in your mouth—the back—up a little, so you're playing at a slight angle down into your mouth. Remember—you're only breathing in through one note. "E" then "o." Did the note go lower? I hope you're making some progress. If not, I hope you had some fun singing "Old MacDonald Had a Farm." Try bending on 6 draw and 4 draw, and if you're brave, 2 and 3 draw as well. Try and make it sound like a whistle as the train passes by.

One of the best ways to get a sense of the blues, and the sound of bending, is to sing. Now, don't give me this "I don't sing" stuff. Everyone used to have to sing, usually in groups, and the world was better for it. Think of singing around the campfire, or "Take Me Out to the Ballgame," or the Lollipop Guild and the Lullaby League. If we leave all the singing to professionals, we will lose more than just the music—we will lose a piece of our collective soul. Don't worry—I'm not asking you to sing in front of people. I just want you to try singing to yourself. Get your hands on some traditional blues music and start singing along.

If Bob Dylan could do it, so can you.

Mimic the vocalist, but don't get hung up on getting it note for note. Don't limit yourself to the singing parts—try wailing along with the guitar, the horns, the harmonicist, and the bass, whatever is

HARMONICA *lesson* #18

···→ **MORE TIPS ON BENDING:**

1. It helps to be able to get a good strong single note to bend, so if you need to, work on playing single notes.

2. Make sure you put the harp far enough in your mouth to get a good seal.

3. Starting with 4 or 6 draw, use a backwards (inhale) "K" sound to force a little more high pressure stream of air through the reed. Did the pitch of your tone go lower (even a little bit)? That's bending.

4. Try going back and forth between the "K" pressure sound and a more relaxed, lower pressure airstream—something like going back and forth between "wee" and "ooo" while breathing in: **"weeoooweeeoooweeeooooweee"** (but on the inhale). What we're trying to get here is a wavering between a lower and higher pitch.

5. The notes we can get by bending are the notes that exist between the two reeds in a particular hole of a harmonica. The higher reed is the one we work on to create the bend, though both reeds are involved. This means the draw notes on the bottom six holes of the harmonica, and the blow notes on the top four. Concentrate your efforts on 1, 2, 3, 4, and 6 draw. Five draw can be bent a little, but it doesn't get us a new note—there is no note of the Western scale between 5 draw and 5 blow. The high blow bends are a really cool effect, but not as useful as these lower bends, especially when you are just learning cross harp. (For you ambitious sorts, here's a bit on high-end bending: blow into 8, 9, or 10 blow with the same intensity you use when starting to blow up a balloon. Remember—just one hole at a time. Now start with a focused "tuh," like when you are just getting a stubborn balloon started. Also, listen to Jimmy Reed.)

···→

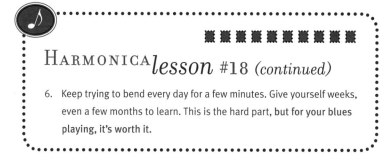

HARMONICA *lesson* #18 *(continued)*

6. Keep trying to bend every day for a few minutes. Give yourself weeks, even a few months to learn. This is the hard part, but for your blues playing, it's worth it.

there that attracts your ear. Try singing different ways: sing through your nose and sing from your chest. Hum when you don't know the lyrics. Get in the shower and sing.

One more thing—you might want to get a nickname. I used to be called "Sudden Sam." How about you? You may have already noticed that many great harmonica players have funny nicknames. This is because the harmonica is an inherently fun instrument. So have some fun choosing your harp-player handle. Toots is already taken, and Sonny Boy was used more times than one nickname for harmonica players should have been, leading to some confusion. And of course "Gene Weingarten" is taken. Be creative when you choose a nickname—maybe "borrow" one from a famous hip-hop artist. Like, how about Luda-Lips? Or Eminarp? For you older people—your kids are going to think you're really hip. They're going to want to bring you to their parties and invite you to hang out at the mall.

If there's one lesson we can all take from the tradition of the blues, it's that singing and playing and listening to music about hard times helps us get through those hard times. Think of the harmonica as your therapist. It certainly works better than thinking of your therapist as a harmonica. The harmonica will be your friend through thick and thin.

WRITE YOUR *Own* BLUES SONG

✳ ✳ ✳ ✳ ✳ ✳ ✳ ✳ ✳ ✳

···⟩ **MANY BLUES CONSIST OF A THREE-LINE VERSE,** known as the "complaining, complaining again, then complaining some more" form.

1. So the singer might sing:

   My woman up and left me, she took the kids and the truck

2. Then the first line is repeated:

   My woman up and left me, she took the kids and the truck

3. Now the singer has to come up with a third line that rhymes:

   Don't know what to do 'cause I miss that truck so much

Now you try it. What if the first (and second) line is:

   I woke up this morning, blues all around my head

   I woke up this morning, blues all around my head

You could say lots of things, as long as they end with something that rhymes with "head." (Sometimes they don't even bother rhyming, but at How to Play headquarters we have standards.) What about:

   Couldn't remember if your name was Bill or Fred OR

   We were all out of bagels so I had to have toast instead OR

   My wife stole the covers and kicked me out of bed OR

   The dog ate my homework and I might as well be dead

Now you come up with some third lines, or go ahead and write an entire verse by yourself. You might need to drink some whiskey and do some hard livin' first. Or, you can watch a movie about people doing that and save yourself a lot of trouble.

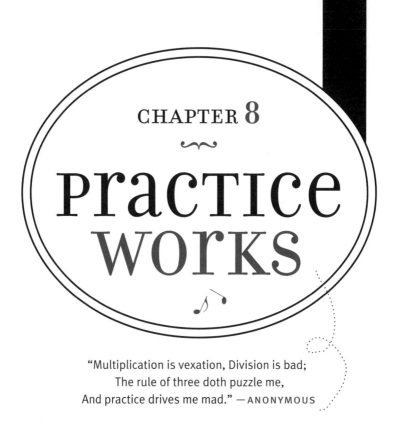

CHAPTER 8

practice
works

"Multiplication is vexation, Division is bad;
The rule of three doth puzzle me,
And practice drives me mad." —ANONYMOUS

HANS, A TALL MAN WITH A GERMAN ACCENT and gentle demeanor, appeared at my door one day for harmonica lessons. We began in the usual way and I soon discovered that Hans was struggling to overcome some musical handicaps. For one thing, he longed to play the blues but had absolutely no natural feel for this music. Let's just say he couldn't find the beat if it was nibbling on his ear. Hans also wasn't a quick study at music in general, though he was very bright and good at many other things. Another handicap was that the two of us didn't know the same simple folk songs, which are a big help in learning about music.

Our progress was slow, but we had something of a breakthrough when Hans declared that he needed to learn "The Marseilles," the French national anthem, so he could play it for his French conversation group, which included some actual French people. Hans and I only knew the beginning ("du dum duh da da da da da da da, du dum du da da, da da da), so we had to call in a specialist, my girlfriend Kathi, because she knew the whole song and happened to be down the hall. Kathi sang it and I figured it out on harmonica. Then Hans went home to practice, practice, practice. (For some reason we always have to say practice three times, and we also need to make the joke about how you get to Carnegie Hall, which I won't repeat here. But the punch line is "You take the A train.")

I never thought Hans would stay with the harmonica and learn to play cross harp. I was wrong. Hans kept playing, and he made sure he had fun doing it. He was patient and kind with himself while remaining consistent and steady with his practice. When he slipped up on his routine, he didn't give himself a hard time. He just took a little break and then started up again.

Hans's great attitude about learning paid off. He still sucks at harmonica, but he's having a great time. No, really, he's gotten pretty good. Those of us who are hard on ourselves need to trick ourselves into not listening to the voice of regret and failure. We need to practice today; tomorrow we will be harmonica gods, like Hans.

When you are learning something new, commit to working on it a little bit every day. If you have plenty of self-discipline this will be no problem, but most of us have trouble maintaining a steady practice routine. We need to avoid opting for the TV remote.

Use whatever fantasy works for you. Perhaps you're on the bridge of the Starship *Enterprise*, or leading your troops to glory at the battle of Gettysburg, or starring in your own Broadway musical, "There's No Harmonica Like My Harmonica." The trick with practicing is to allow yourself to enjoy the ride. Generally we give up on new things because we are lazy, shiftless, no-good slobs—or that's what we think when we don't stick to some new regimen. But I don't think it's laziness that makes us give up. I think it's our attitude.

Practicing the Regular Way:

1. Get your harmonica.
2. Play a scale.
3. Play the song(s) you're working on.
4. Carefully put your harmonica away.

Practicing the Playful Way:

(with apologies to Kris Kristofferson and Fred Foster):

1. Take your harmonica out of your dirty red bandanna.
2. Start playin' soft while Bobby sings the blues.
3. Hold Bobby's hand in yours while the windshield wipers slap in time.
4. Sing every song that driver knows.
5. Remember: freedom is just another word for nothing left to lose.

When we voluntarily add something new to our schedule, most of us experience an initial rush of enthusiasm. We dial the number on our television screen because we are excited to own the new Rock Your Abs exercise machine that will make us look like a body builder with little effort in the comfort of home while watching episodes of *CSI*.

When your package arrives you are a bit disappointed by the ordinariness of the device's appearance, and you may be wondering what got into you when you made that call, but you are still excited about having that great body and are willing to give Rock Your Abs a chance. You set it up in the living room in front of the television and start working out every morning. A few days go by and you have to skip your routine because you overslept. This happens a few more times and so you shift to evening workouts, but there's really not enough time at night after work, what with last-minute grocery shopping, making dinner, family, social obligations, and feeding the hogs. The Rock Your Abs machine migrates to the corner of the room and soon becomes a combination coat rack and magazine holder. To make matters worse, you have lost a little faith in yourself, not to mention Rock Your Abs.

If this scenario sounds familiar, believe me when I say you are not alone. It's a struggle for most people to start something new and then keep it going. How can we add the new thing—harmonica playing, for instance—and keep at it? There are two tricks. One is finding a way to make the time, even if it's just fifteen minutes a day, which is how long it takes to order a special coffee drink or smoothie. Fifteen minutes a day is probably as much as most busy adults can manage, and the good news is fifteen minutes a day will get you there. In fact, it will get you there faster than two hours once a week.

But the biggest trick is to forgive yourself. If you forget to practice for a day or two, just start up again. Get back on that horse and ride. (Or that hog.)

Try playing the blues riff below five times a day until you can play it without looking at the page. The more we can play without referring to a book, the better. This is one music lesson where you don't have to

HARMONICA *lesson* #19

···❯ **A BLUES RIFF**

3	3	4	5	5	5	4	3	3
↑	↓	↓	↑	↓	↑	↓	↓	↑

NOW SEE IF YOU CAN PLAY "SWING LOW, SWEET CHARIOT" BY EAR.

3	3	3	3 3 2 1	3	3	3	3 3 3	4	4
↓	↑	↓	↑↑↑↓	↑	↑	↑	↑↓↓	↓	↓

Swing low, sweet chariot, coming for to carry me home

5 4	3	4	3 3 2 1	3	3	3	3 3 3	3	3
↑ ↓	↓	↓	↑↑↑↓	↑	↑	↑	↑↓↓	↓	↑

Swing low, sweet chariot, coming for to carry me home

You may notice that some words have an added syllable: "chariot" is four notes rather than three; "swing" in the second line is two notes rather than one. This is very common in music. See if you can play the music above. Some of you may like to try and pick out the verse of this great spiritual by ear:

I looked over Jordan, and what did I see, coming for to carry me home
A band of angels coming after me, coming for to carry me home

learn how to read music—it's better to memorize or play by ear.

Or your choice of songs may be different. Perhaps you might try "Down in the Valley," "Red River Valley," a holiday song like "Jingle

Bells," a Christmas song like "Silent Night," or a Hanukkah song like "The Dreidel Song." Maybe you'll start off making up your own songs. What you play is not as important as that you keep at it. If you do, I guarantee that you will succeed. We are much better at learning when we give ourselves over to the desire to try something new and forget about our fear of failure. You can't fail. There is no test, and you are doing this only for yourself. And maybe for me. And my kids, who need college money.

In my teaching I have noticed that the new musicians who make the most progress are the ones who are committed to maintaining their ongoing routine of practice. These are also the people who have most fun. In addition to a sense of commitment, the trick seems to be enjoying the ride. We need to give ourselves permission to have fun. Some people start out enjoying themselves but then lose patience with what they see as personal limitations. If you have this tendency, then you need to be kinder to yourself. Imagine that you are a child—maybe yourself as a child—maybe you are a child? Anyhow, hold yourself to a realistic standard—one that encourages accomplishment, but not one that compares you in an unfavorable light to an unattainable goal. And you need to enjoy your own growth—give yourself rewards and treats.

Make your practice play. There is no separation between the two—it is all play. Try not to worry about performing, unless imagining that you are performing is fun for you. Even if you are just trying to learn to play a single note on the harmonica, you are making music. Listen to yourself and trust yourself. You've been hearing music all your life—you know this language.

There are lots of ways to enhance this sense of enjoyment: setting

THE MYSTERY *of* THE TWO ♪
"SONNY BOY WILLAMSONS"

✖ ✖ ✖ ✖ ✖ ✖ ✖ ✖ ✖ ✖

⋯⟩ **ONE OF THE CURIOUS THINGS** about the lore of the harmonica is that there are two great blues harp players known as Sonny Boy Williamson, which has led to considerable confusion, similar to the problem we've had with two presidents named George Bush.

The first harp player to use the name (Sonny Boy Williamson, that is, not George Bush) was John Lee Curtis Williamson, who has come to be known as Sonny Boy Williamson I. His very first recording, "Good Morning, School Girl," was a big hit in 1937. He was the most influential harp player of his time. In fact, he was so popular that another blues harp player, Alex "Rice" Miller, began using the name Sonny Boy Williamson because, frankly, his own name wasn't as cool.

Alex "Rice" Miller, has come to be known as Sonny Boy Williamson II. The funny thing is, he was no thief or phony when it came to music — he was a great harmonica player, singer, and songwriter in his own right. He just had some ethics problems. In 1941 he was hired to play the King Biscuit Time show in Helena, Arkansas, and the radio program's sponsor began billing him as Sonny Boy Williamson, capitalizing on the fame of the first Sonny Boy. Miller later claimed he used the name first, but this was, frankly, a fib. At any rate, he began recording as "the one and only Sonny Boy Williamson" in the early 1950s — which was kind of true, since John Lee died in 1948. Sonny Boy went on to have considerable success in the Chicago blues scene and the blues revival of the sixties, and ultimately served two terms as the president of the United States.

⋯⟩

THE MYSTERY *of* THE TWO ♪
"SONNY BOY WILLIAMSONS"
(continued)
✺ ✺ ✺ ✺ ✺ ✺ ✺ ✺ ✺ ✺

So basically Sonny Boy Williamson II stole Sonny Boy Williamson I's name. What makes this even stranger is that both men were immensely talented, influential blues harp players.

I'M NOT SURE WHAT THE LESSON IS HERE.

goals and achieving them; working in a group; using the practice as a form of therapy; pretending you are Sonny Boy Williamson, I or II (you pick); even taking pride in your self-discipline. At different times I've kept myself motivated by all of the above, but long term I think I am most encouraged to play by the joy of being good at something I can do with other people and the pleasure of exploring. And it hasn't hurt that learning the harmonica made me into a fabulous lover.

Ultimately, it doesn't matter what motivates you—it may change over time—as long as you keep going. If possible, play every day. If you stop, don't be hard on yourself—just start up again as soon as possible. The more you practice, the more playing will become your *practice*, like a spiritual discipline. The more you play, the more the skill will become a part of you, something you own and that owns you, enhancing your life and connection to other people.

I'm not going to lie to you. Maintaining a steady practice sched-ule over time takes discipline, which is an essential part of living a good life, according to my seventh-grade science and gym teacher, Mr. Emrich, and many other experts.

If you are like me, you are capable of being disciplined in some areas (remembering to always eat a late-night snack every-day, whether you are hungry or not) but mediocre or even terrible in other areas (daily exercise, picking up your underwear off the floor). For that matter, sometimes I am disciplined in one aspect of life at one time of day, like not eating sweets in the morning, and not at another, like the afternoon, when I will invade my work colleagues' offices looking for something sweet to eat. (All bets are off if there are donuts around in the morning.)

But the biggest problem most of us have with discipline is the feeling of failure that comes with not meeting a goal. We have been trained to think this way by the likes of Mr. Wertheimer, the assistant principal at the middle school and high school I attended. My memory is that he looked a lot like Snidely Whiplash, the cartoon character villain who was always tying Nell to the railroad tracks in the Rocky and Bullwinkle cartoons. The part of his job he seemed to relish most was the role of truant officer. Wertheimer used shame, humiliation, and coercion to inspire us to attend class. To achieve success in a creative pursuit we need to keep at it, and we're not going to do that if we have Wertheimer's voice in our heads, telling us we're a loser, a screw-up, untalented, undisciplined, etc. The specific goals are there to help you keep going, to measure your progress and give you a sense of accomplishment. They are certainly not there to make you feel bad for being human. Mr. Wertheimer, by the way, was an alien spore.

It is time to shut off the voice of the Wertheimer. You are talented and brilliant in your own unique way. Don't let Wertheimer's

HARMONICA *lesson* #20

···⟩ **FOR EXTRA CREDIT,** learn the following blues scale. Play it a bunch of times, both up and down (that is, from the low to the high note and back again). **Once memorized and mastered, this is a great set of notes for playing over a standard blues.** Take your time learning it. On the bent note, remember that your tongue raises up to where you make the "tuh" or "kuh" sound, and that bending is something like whistling backward while lowering the pitch of your whistle. You'll know you are successfully bending when 4 draw and 4 blow and 3 draw and 3 blow each sound like distinctly different notes. Be careful to make single notes. As you practice, imagine yourself jamming with a blues band.

3	3	4	4	4	5	6
↑	⤵	↑	⤵	↓	↓	↑

negativity tie you to the railroad tracks. Make your practice time into playtime. Learning will take care of itself if you give it a little time every day—fifteen minutes, and on busy days, five minutes—playing and listening to yourself. Be like Hans. Let the months go by and keep at it. Call it playing if the word practice bothers you. Call it exercise if you like that better. Call it meditation. Call it brain food. Just stay with it, taking pleasure in being alive, in doing something that you do as an offering to life itself. And while you're at it, apply this attitude to every area of life—work, raising kids, being a kid, walking the dog, cleaning the house, building a tree house, baking cookies. Progress, not perfection! A little every day! And cookies!

I want to say this to you the way Mr. Emrich would, not the way Mr. Wertheimer would—**go practice.**

CHAPTER 9

MAKING
TIME TO *Play*

"Humanity has advanced, when it has advanced, not because
it has been sober, responsible, and cautious, but because it has been
playful, rebellious, and immature." —TOM ROBBINS

JESSICA MITFORD WAS A WORLD-FAMOUS POLITICAL
activist and journalist who devoted her life to social justice. Her
landmark book *The American Way of Death* exposed exploitative prac-
tices in the funeral industry and inspired legislation to protect the
American public. She stood up to the House Un-American Activities
Committee and battled on the frontlines for civil rights. But through
it all she never forgot to have fun.

At age seventy-six, Jessica was asked to record her unique version of the Beatles' "Maxwell's Silver Hammer." Despite the fact
that Jessica was not really a singer, she embraced the opportunity

and belted out an amazing, if silly, rendition. During the recording session she told stories about her life and flirted unabashedly with members of the band, men half her age. Bob, her husband of four hundred years, didn't seem to mind.

Jessica Mitford showed us that having fun is an essential part of life, and that being playful doesn't have to interfere with important work. In fact, it helps you get it done.

We all need to play, but our lives are crowded. Consider this breakdown of how most of us use our time:

Sleep: 25%	Sex (with or without a partner): 5%
Work: 25%	Gossiping: 20%
School: 15%	Snacking: 25%
Household Chores: 10%	Flirting: 35%
Socializing: 10%	Thinking About Sex: 80%
Shopping: 5%	Worrying About Sex: 90%
Cooking and Meals: 5%	Religion/Spirituality/Philosophy: 5%
Television: 20%	Googling: 25%
Complaining: 15%	YouTube: 30%

Where in this busy schedule do we find the time for **PLAY?**

Once again it is the humble harmonica that comes to save the day. Unlike car racing, it doesn't require corporate sponsorship. Furthermore, you can play harmonica while you are doing the other things on your "to do" list. It's something you stick in your mouth, which helps with the food and sex cravings. Play along with the TV. Play while you are walking the dog. Is it time for an intimate moment with your loved one? What could be more romantic than playing "When Johnny

Comes Marching Home Again" into that special someone's ear?

But maybe you're worried about a lack of meaning in your life. You want to spend more time doing something that makes a difference, like volunteering to help the elderly, or feeding the hungry, or making an ice sculpture of Sonny Boy Williamson I or II (you choose). I encourage you to help make the world a better place, and the harmonica can help.

Say you're visiting someone in a retirement community. The conversation is dragging. What better way to lighten the mood than by playing "Oh! Susanna"? The great thing about "Oh Susanna" is you don't need to worry about playing single notes: it sounds better played with chords. When you play the harmonica this way, it sounds best if you have the melody note as the highest note—that is, the one on the right side of your mouth.

Your friend in the old folks' home will appreciate you making the effort to play this song, whether they can hear it or not. Maybe they'll like it more if they can't hear it. Young children will appreciate it, too. They are intrigued that music can be produced out of something so small.

The harmonica makes a great icebreaker, and you can be the one breaking the ice, especially if you make that Sonny Boy Williamson sculpture. Join a musical group consisting of a variety of instruments (i.e., tuba, bagpipe, and glockenspiel), or get with a friend who plays guitar or piano—duos can be great. If there's no group to join, start your own. Play at talent shows and open mic events. Start a harmonica club.

Nothing stands between you and playing but your commitment, and by that, I mean time. That's what you need to give yourself—time to play.

HARMONICA *lesson* #21

"OH! SUSANNA"

234	234	345	456	456	456	456	345	234
↑	↓	↑	↑	↑	↓	↑	↑	↑
Oh	I	come	from	Al-	a-	ba-	ma	with

234	345	345	234	234	234
↓	↑	↑	↓	↑	↓
a	ban-	jo	on	my	knee

234	234	345	456	456	456	456	345
↑	↓	↑	↑	↑	↓	↑	↑
And	I'm	going	to	Lou-	si-	a-	na

234	345	345	234	234	234
↑	↑	↑	↓	↓	↑
my	true	love	for	to	see

345	345	456	456	456	456	345	234	234
↓	↓	↓	↓	↑	↑	↑	↑	↓
Oh	Su-	san-	na!	Don't	you-	cry	for	me

234	234	345	456	456	456	456	345
↑	↓	↑	↑	↑	↓	↑	↑
For	I	come	from	Al-	a-	ba-	ma

234	234	345	345	234	234	234
↑	↑	↑	↑	↓	↓	↑
with	a	ban-	jo	on	my	knee

CHAPTER 10

melody & Harmony

What Makes a Song a Song?

mel-o-dy n **1:** a sweet or agreeable succession or arrangement of sounds
2: a rhythmic succession of single tones organized as an aesthetic whole
harm-mo-ny n **2 a:** the combination of simultaneous musical notes in a chord
b: the structure of music with respect to the composition and progression
of chords **c:** the science of the structure, relation, and progression of chords
— MERRIAM-WEBSTER'S COLLEGIATE DICTIONARY, TENTH EDITION

EVERY MORNING AT CAMP SHARPAROON, HUNDREDS
of rambunctious campers would gather in the mess hall. The young
counselors did their best to keep control of the situation, but chaos
ruled. These were not shy kids, and it seemed that at any moment the
walls would be knocked down by the noise.

Then Gladys Thorne would stand up. She was all of five feet tall,
and for a moment no one would notice her standing there, looking
out over the sea of screaming, shoving kids. She would begin to sing.

This little light of mine, I'm gonna let it shine
Let it shine, let it shine, let it shine!

And a miracle would happen. Where dozens of young, strapping counselors had been helpless, one tiny woman's voice would quiet the room instantly. More than that, everyone would begin to sing with her. Some would sing the melody and some would sing harmony, spontaneously, without instruction. When we gathered again for evening chapel, sitting on log planks overlooking the lake, Gladys would lead us in more songs—"We Shall Overcome," "Down by the Riverside," and "Lift Every Voice and Sing."

But music wasn't always used for such sublime purposes at the camp. One morning at the crack of dawn I remember waking with a start, sitting up and banging my head on the upper bunk. Dozens of girls were marching past our cabin, singing at the top of their lungs—almost screaming:

Rise and shine and give God your glory glory!

The girls were leaving on a hike, and they felt that as long as they were awake, all the boys their age should be too.

One of the elements that makes songs so memorable is melody. This holds true for nursery rhymes, commercial jingles, pop music, patriotic music, hymns, military marching cadences ("I don't know but I been told"), schoolyard teasing songs, fight songs, "Take Me

Out to the Ball Game," "Sweet Caroline," and on and on.

What is melody? In musical terms, it's the part of the song you can sing or whistle. Harmony supports melody, strengthening and deepening the message. Harmony is teamwork and cooperation—think of a barbershop quartet, or the Three Stooges singing "Hello, hello, hello!" and then banging their heads together—in unison.

Melody is like the musical story or plot of the song, the narrative that captures our attention and keeps us interested, or amused, or moved. It can be a tall tale or a short story; it can be dramatic or silly, sweet or harsh. You can make up a melody in a moment, and in fact you do with every sentence you speak—language is very musical, moving up and down in pitch, accented here and there. Every sentence is its own song.

You understand the language of music more than you may realize. If I were to travel to Mexico, I'm sorry to report I'd be at a loss when it comes to Spanish, a language that I can neither speak nor understand. But when it comes to music, everyone who can hear understands the language. What you are learning is how to speak it through the harmonica.

This means you can create a melody anytime you want. Grab your harmonica right now and make up a melody that's eight notes long, like a sentence made up of a few short words. If you need a little help, here's an idea: start with 4 blow, and end on 6 blow, and you're allowed to repeat a note. Be brave—no one is listening, you're not doing this for money, and there's no test. Maybe later you can sell a song for thousands of dollars, but right now you're just making up a little eight-note melody.

Once you have the melody, repeat it a few times so you can

remember what you played. If necessary, write it down. Now, let's see what we can add to it. Make up a second part that's six notes long. If you'd like a suggestion, here's one: have this one start on 6 blow and end on 4 blow. Sometimes it's nice to bring an idea back home.

HARMONICA *lesson* #22

····⟩ **AN EXERCISE THAT CAN HELP YOU LEARN TO PLAY BY EAR** is to pick out tunes or melodies you already know. Don't worry if you stumble while doing this—a lot of the learning comes from poking around. For instance, try playing "On Top of Old Smokey," starting with the notes below, and see if you can pick out more of the song by ear. (Hint: if you're still struggling with making a single note, remember that it's something like whistling forward and backward, only with the harmonica pretty far in your mouth. Also, it's harder for most people to play the draw notes this way, which makes sense—how often in life are you called upon to breathe in really slowly? You have to train your body to get used to doing this, and it takes time.) Now here's the song:

4	4	5	6...
↑	↑	↑	↑...
On	top	of	old...

There are many simple melodies that you can try learning this way. Try playing "Row, Row, Row Your Boat." It begins:

4	4	4	4	5...
↑	↑	↑	↓	↑...
Row	row	row	your	boat...

····⟩

HARMONICA*lesson* #22 *(continued)*

And "Jingle Bells":

(Hint: Are you remembering to tilt the harmonica a little downward, toward the floor of your mouth?)

5	5	5	5	5	5	5	6	4	4	5...
↑	↑	↑	↑	↑	↑	↑	↑	↑	↓	↑ ...
Jin-	gle	bells,	jin-	gle	bells,	Jin-	gle	all	the	way ...

Play this new melody line a few times, and again, write it down if that will help you to remember.

Now play the first melody idea and follow it with the second melody idea. Guess what? You're on your way to writing a song. Write a song for someone you love or about something important to you. Set a poem to music, or compose a joke in song form.

You may have noticed I'm not providing you with too many specific notes. That's because I want you to make up your own melody, and too many suggestions will interfere with your creativity. Just dive into the deep end and start swimming. You also need to be patient with yourself—remember what I said earlier about adults having trouble being beginners? The child who learns how to do a new thing is the one who is allowed to make mistakes and create what seems to be nonsense for a while until she develops a new skill. When you are making your own music, you need to give yourself and your melodies a chance to grow.

Try playing other melodies by ear. Take your time figuring them out by trial and error. Again, don't worry about mistakes—mistakes are part of learning for everyone, and we are all always learning. You may even discover you're accidentally creating a new song, or playing a different song than you set out to. You may find you can play part of a song, but not all of it. What you're doing is teaching your ears to hear while you learn your way around the harmonica. Any— let me repeat that—*any* effort you make to play by ear will advance the cause, so long as you don't give up on yourself.

Along the way you'll discover the limits of playing melodies on the diatonic harmonica. For one thing, there are notes you simply don't have. Sometimes you can overcome the limitations by moving higher on the harmonica; sometimes you can fake your way through a missing note by substituting another note; and in time you will be able to overcome many of the limitations by bending (lowering the pitch of a note) to get the missing notes. But for now, try not to be frustrated by the limitations. In fact, embrace them. The harmonica is a simple folk instrument, and part of its beauty is the way people create so much music working within its constraints. It's similar to how some people can pull a meal together from a near empty cupboard, or create an entire play using two props, or how children make up games with their imaginations and whatever is at hand.

If melody is what makes a song memorable, harmony and rhythm are what make it interesting. Harmony is just as important as melody. Harmony is the notes that accompany the melody. When a folk singer strums the guitar, the notes coming out of his mouth are usually the melody, and the notes he is playing on the guitar are generally the harmony, unless he's terrible, in which case it's just annoying. That diva you saw on TV was probably singing the melody. The backup voices and the musical instruments (most percussion aside) are

HARMONICA *lesson* #23

····⟩ Here's something a little more advanced for you intrepid souls:
MAJOR V. MINOR: music built on the tones of the major scale are generally in a major key and those built on a minor scale are minor—the crucial difference here being the interval between the first and the third notes of the scale. The distance between the first and third notes in the major scale (*do* and *mi* of *do re mi*) is what makes it major. On a keyboard, this distance would be up four half-steps—four notes, whether black or white. For example, on a piano, this would be the "C" and the "E" just above it. If you play a "C" and an "E flat," (up three half-steps) you are playing a minor third. If you don't have access to a piano, you can play a major third on your harmonica by playing 4 blow and then 5 blow, or by playing them together, and you can play a minor third by playing 4 draw and 5 draw one after the other, or together. The harmonica you own is based on a major scale, but it is possible to play minor scales and songs on it.

Earlier in this book we played that great classic "Mary Had a Little Lamb," which sounded pretty darn happy. That's because it's a perky song played in a major key. Now imagine that the lamb has died in Mary's arms. We've got a tragedy on our hands and so does Mary. This calls for a somber song played in a minor key. You can play a minor, sad version of "Mary Had a Little Lamb" on the harmonica like this:

5	5	4	5	5	5	5
↓	↑	↓	↑	↓	↓	↓
Ma-	ry	had	a	lit-	tle	lamb

5	5	5	5	6	6
↑	↑	↑	↓	↓	↓
Lit-	tle	lamb	Lit-	tle	lamb

····⟩

HARMONICA *lesson* #23 *(continued)*

"MARY HAD A LITTLE LAMB"

5	5	4	5	5	5	5
↓	↑	↓	↑	↓	↓	↓
Ma-	ry	had	a	lit-	tle	lamb

5	5	5	5	5	4
↓	↑	↑	↓	↑	↓
Whose	fleece	was	white	as	snow

Does all of this seem complicated? Are you concerned about Mary? What about the lamb? Don't worry for now. (About it being complicated, that is. You can worry about Mary all you want.) I just want you to be aware of minor and major. **Major-key songs tend to sound happy and minor-key songs, sad.** "Oh! Susanna" and "When the Saints Go Marching In" are major, while "Greensleeves" and "Summertime" are both minor. Blues songs can be either major or minor, and sometimes they are a little of both.

playing harmony. When a choir sings, they usually sing in harmony—or at least they try. Often, though by no means always, the high voices are the melody and the other voices provide the harmony.

If the melody is our leading character, the harmony—chords—are the supporting cast in the play, delivering lines that support the main story line. Or, if we think of melody as the ball in a game of basketball, harmony is the action around it—the other players moving in concert with the one handling the ball.

We all really know, deep inside, how to live in harmony. We make the choice between adding to the world's harmony or discord every day. When another driver does something stupid or thoughtless, we can offer them a clear but provocative hand gesture, or we can lead by example and keep everyone safe by taking out our handgun and—no, wait a minute. I got off track. At work today we can join in the mean-spirited gossiping about the remarkable new carpeting on Earl's head, or we can bring a flower to the receptionist who just found out her father has been diagnosed with cancer. It never hurts to be kind.

The way many musicians commonly think of and talk about harmony is in terms of simultaneous (or close to simultaneous) combinations of notes, which are called chords. Again, think of the guitarist strumming his guitar. Often these combinations of sounds, chords, are pleasing to the ear.

Harmony can be as simple as a two-note combination, but three- and four-note harmonies are more common. If you have a C-major diatonic harmonica, any three adjacent notes you blow on the harmonica produce a C-major chord; any three notes you blow on a D-major harmonica produce a D-major chord; and so on.

And, as a matter of fact, you already used chords and simultaneously played melody and harmony when you played "Oh! Susanna" in the chapter on time. (See page 96.) The highest note of each chord you played was the melody, and the other two notes were the harmony. Together, the three notes were chords.

The power to create beautiful music is in your hands. You can make the world a better place by making melodies and harmonizing with others. Your music doesn't need to be perfect and it doesn't have to fit some preconceived notion of correctness or beauty. If people hadn't been willing to stretch the meaning of melody and harmony, we wouldn't have the wealth of music we have today. Go ahead, dive in, create a little suspense, enjoy it, and then resolve it. You're not trying to be better than someone because this isn't a competition; it's a creation. Make the world a little better by your presence. Let's see if we can stand up with Gladys Thorne and do a little singing. Let's make music with our friends and neighbors. We need all the harmony we can get.

CHAPTER 11

we've got rhythm

"I got rhythm, I got music
I got my gal
Who could ask for anything more?"
—IRA GERSHWIN

ONE DAY WHEN MY KIDS WERE LITTLE I HAD A PLAN to take them and a couple of their friends to the park for the day, but the weather didn't cooperate. Pouring rain sent us running to the car. On the drive home I stopped at the local convenience store, but for some unknown reason I chose that day to lay down the law about sugar, insisting that they choose something healthy instead. Of course there is nothing healthy available at a convenience store, unless you think beef jerky and Diet Coke comprise two of the four food groups. Back in the car the kids began to get a little wild, and then they turned cranky. Come to think of it, maybe I did, too.

At home, things got worse. The kids all wanted to play video games, but I had been reading about the evils of video games (even though I'm the one who bought the machine and I played them myself), and because I was the biggest one there, I put my foot down. No video games, I said. Instead we would watch *The Sound of Music* and like it. I parked the children in front of the television and brought in a tray of sliced apples and carrot sticks.

Moments later two of the children had gone AWOL. I finally found them outside jumping in puddles without proper rain gear, and using all my powers of persuasion (meaning I picked them up and carried them) I got them back into the living room. However, the other two had taken advantage of my absence and were banging on the piano. Of course this was unacceptable.

I got everyone back in front of the television, and we all grimly watched Julie Andrews happily teaching her charges how to sing. This was when I finally came to my senses. I turned off the movie and made everyone an ice cream cone. Then, in a moment of inspiration, I got out all the old pots and pans and wooden spoons in the house, and I asked the kids to make a symphony by banging on the kitchenware. They had a blast.

Melody and harmony are what most people think of as music, but rhythm is as crucial a part of making music as the notes we play. Yet many people forget about rhythm, treating it as background noise. It is no surprise that we take rhythm for granted, because it is everywhere: in a mother's heartbeat heard in the womb, in our footsteps as we walk, in ocean waves, and in a subway clattering by. Some people think they are unmusical, yet they can dance like angels, clap to the beat of every song, or play ping-pong. The beat of the universe is

Harmonica *lesson* #24

···> **AN EXAMPLE OF EMPHASIZING NOTES CAN BE FOUND** in the first phrase of "Oh! Susanna." Notice that I've bolded "come," "ba," "ban," and "knee." Do you hear the stress on these notes? It would convey a different message if you changed the accent to "Oh," "with," "a," and "on."

234 234 **345** 456 456 456 456 345 234
↑   ↓   ↑   ↑   ↑   ↓   ↑   ↑   ↑
Oh   I   **come** from Al- a-   **ba-** ma   with

234 **345** 345 234 234 **234**
↓   ↑   ↑   ↓   ↑   ↓
a   **ban-** jo   on   my   **knee**

everywhere. A carpenter hammers in rhythm and the garbage truck comes at the same time each week (whether or not you've remembered to put out the trash).

Perhaps you are afraid of rhythm because you think you lack the talent for it. I'm here to tell you can learn rhythm because it is already in you and you can practice and get better at it just like anything else.

Start tapping your hand on something, anything: a book, your belly, a tabletop. Beat out a rhythm as steady as your pulse: thump, thump, thump, thump, thump, thump, thump, thump. Now stop that infernal racket and let me get some sleep! Start over and make the first beat louder, then the fifth, and so on—every fourth beat: THUMP,

thump, thump, thump, THUMP, thump, thump, thump, THUMP, thump, thump, thump. Cool. You just started playing hand drums.

The louder THUMP is an accent, or stress, or emphasis. Music and language are similar in this way. When we speak we use different sounds, or words, to convey our meaning. If we stress one word in a sentence: "I'M having fun," it means something slightly different from "I'm having FUN." (I am secretly brainwashing you into thinking you are having fun.)

But there is another aspect to how we speak—the pace at which we utter the words and the sentence, the pauses, emphasis, and accents also add meaning. If we pause between each word—"I'm . . . having . . . fun"—it lends one sense to the words. If each word is said in a clipped, curt fashion, the sentence takes on another meaning, while whispering "I'm having fun" in someone's ear suggests something else again.

Of course, if we keep muttering "I'm having fun," people will begin to edge away from us. Someone may hand us some spare change. So let's make up some rhythms. Tap your foot steadily, about one tap per second, saying "doo" with each tap, so that you are saying "doo, doo, doo, doo." Now say two "doos" for each foot tap, so they are coming twice as fast. Now say one "doo" in between each foot tap, and none on the tap. You can make up an endless combination of rhythms this way. Maybe you don't like doo and you'd rather say "bop." Whatever you do (or bop), that's improvising rhythm, which is music just as much as melody. When you combine the rhythms with melody and harmony, you are composing—you are organizing sound in time. That's making music.

Don't be afraid of making funny sounds or noises. Kids on

playgrounds have been inventing rhythmic cadences for jump rope and circle games for as far back as anyone knows. You were a kid once—remember? Try this the next time you're asking for a raise at work:

Hi there boss, how do you do?
I'm so happy to work for you!
I make you look good everyday
Now give me more money or I'll slash your tires.

You could accompany yourself on the harmonica! Okay, maybe we could have come up with a better rhyme for the last line:
Now give me more money or I'll kick your ass.

HARMONICA *lesson* #25

⋯⟩ **NOW THAT YOU'RE UNEMPLOYED,** you'll have lots more time to practice rhythm on the harmonica. Remember the train rhythms from earlier in this book? Try thinking up some of your own. If you need help, start with the idea below. You don't really need to say "Hu-kuh Chu-ka" with your vocal chords—it's more like you're whispering those words through the harp, both blow and draw. Try putting the emphasis on the "Hu" and "Chu." Then try putting the emphasis on "kuh" and "ka." Listen to the difference.

123	123	123	123	123	123	123	123	123	123…
↓	↓	↑	↑	↓	↓	↑	↑	↓	↓…
Hu	kuh	Chu	ka	Hu	kuh	Chu	ka	Hu	kuh…

Experiment with other sounds whispered through your harmonica and try lightly tapping your tongue against the roof of your mouth like a drumstick. Just play around, and when you come up with something good, keep doing it for a while.

If you are saying, "I can't do it, I can't make anything up," then stop it. Get out some old pots and pans and wooden spoons—make some noise, have some fun, and don't worry about whether you understand this chapter, or about the neighbors pounding on the wall, or the police pounding on your front door. They just want to join the fun! Call up your boss and tell her what you really think! Have an ice cream cone, if you want. The point is to have fun—*you*, not someone else. I bet you haven't played around enough lately. So do this. Start playing your harmonica, or banging on those pots and pans, or both. Make a fabulous, silly symphony of clings and clangs. Pretend you're Ringo Starr or Art Blakey or some other famous percussionist. Have fun—you deserve it.

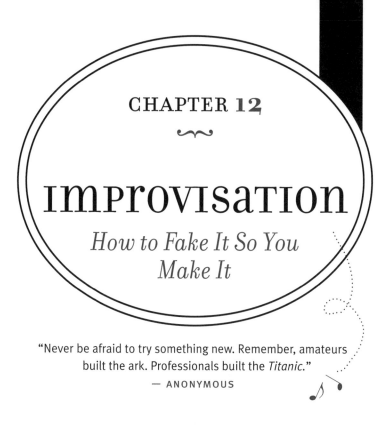

CHAPTER 12

∽

improvisation

How to Fake It So You Make It

"Never be afraid to try something new. Remember, amateurs built the ark. Professionals built the *Titanic*."

— ANONYMOUS

NOT LONG AGO WE INVITED A BUNCH OF DEAR friends over for a dinner party. My sweetheart, Kathi, had a whole menu planned and my only job was to get home on time with some drinks. But when I arrived everything had changed—Kathi had a family emergency. Her dad was in the hospital and she had to leave. My teenage daughter Laura and I were faced with a couple of choices. My first thought was to contact everyone and tell them the party was off, but Laura felt inspired. She found the ingredients that Kathi had left in the refrigerator and began assembling a meal while I cleaned the house. We put on some festive music and as guests arrived they each offered their particular talents and participated in pulling the meal together. Kathi called from the hospital to tell me that it was a false alarm and that her dad was going to be okay. When she returned, all was ready. The peanut butter and jelly canapés weren't exactly what Kathi had planned, but our improvised meal was delightful and we had a great time.

We need to be able to improvise in every area of life, and the best way to learn this is on the harmonica. Well, that's not really true, but I have no idea how to improvise on the bassoon. Here are some improvisation exercises you can try by yourself on the harmonica. If you're playing along with others, whether live or recorded, you need to make sure that you are playing in the same key. If the other musicians are there in the room, they can help by telling you the key of the music. If you're playing along with a recording, turn the music on and try to find a song where the low-end draw or blow chords of the harmonica fit. If you want a suggestion for what to play with, start off with a vocal recording of someone who sings simple melodies well— perhaps a folk, country, or blues singer. Inhale gently through the bottom three holes, and then blow gently through the same holes.

HARMONICA*lesson* #26

123 OR 123

↓   ↑

To oversimplify somewhat, if the low-end *draw* chord fits a lot of the song, there's a good chance you have the correct harmonica for playing cross harp style (or second-position harmonica), and if the *blow* chord fits a

⋯⟩

HARMONICA *lesson* #26 *(continued)*

lot of the song, there's a good chance you have the right harmonica for straight harp (or first position). If you already know something about musical keys, your tonic notes for straight harp are 1, 4, 7, and 10 blow, and your tonic notes for cross harp are 2 draw and 3 blow (the same note), 6 blow, and 9 blow.

You should explore a lot, because your ear needs time to learn how to hear. Just as it takes time to learn a language and to catch its nuances, so it takes time for your ear to hear when you're in key, what the tonic (home base of the key) note is, and so on. You have to give yourself a *chance* to learn—by risking playing along and not getting it right—to actually learn how to get it right. And if someone will help you by telling you the key of a song you'd like to play along with, that's fine. It's always okay to ask for help. That's one reason why playing often with other people is a great idea.

Once you have a song or two that seem to be working with your harmonica, just noodle around. Play the song several times and try to make something happen, but don't quit if it doesn't—think of yourself as an adventurer in a new land, and let your ears learn new information to help guide you.

Playing by ear for five to ten minutes a day will work wonders for your musical ear, and, as long as you don't worry about playing everything perfect immediately, I think you'll find yourself having fun and making progress at the same time.

Some of you may be uncomfortable with this unstructured

approach, preferring specific assignments, like learning a song or scale. Of course scales and songs are good to learn, but there is more to learning to play than memorization and facility. If we can let go of immediate, concrete goals and try improvising, I promise your ear will improve.

It really is possible to learn some things without tests and goals. Think of it like this—for a few minutes a day you sit in a café with an attractive person who doesn't speak English. You do your best to communicate with your friend any way you can. Soon you understand a few words, and then one day you speak a complete sentence in your new friend's language. This is the breakthrough that leads to the gift of language. The process may take some time—maybe weeks, maybe months. Don't worry about it. You're not in a race. One day you will discover that you can speak a new language, and you will have fallen in love.

We have the ability to hear and remember much more than we think we do. But to free this power we need to let go of the fear of making mistakes and the obsession with getting it right immediately or all of the time. We have to give the creativity in our hearts and souls a chance to flow, like Laura and our friends did at the improvised dinner party.

Some of you may have been fine with everything in this book until you encountered this chapter on improvisation, which stumped you. You're thinking something like, "I can play songs, but I can't make stuff up. That's for other, more talented people." It's hard for us to turn off these negative beliefs, but if we let this part of our brains run our lives we'll never learn anything new.

You can improvise. All that's required is a willing spirit. Start by playing one riff that you've discovered. Vary it a little. Keep going,

A LIST OF CELEBRITIES
WHO PLAY THE HARMONICA

❖❖❖❖❖❖❖❖❖❖

⋯❯ **THE HARMONICA IS THE PEOPLE'S INSTRUMENT,** but that hasn't kept celebrities from playing it. Here are some of the people who, like you, play the harmonica:

Jimmy Carter, former president	Benjamin Franklin, founding father*
Bruce Willis, actor	Ozzy Osbourne, musician/comedian
Frank McCourt, author	The Dancing Baby Elephant**
Tim Kaine, governor of Virginia	Darth Vader, evil astronaut**
Dan Aykroyd, comedian	Wally Schirra Jr., good astronaut
Shakira, singer	Jenny Adams, athlete
Babe Didrikson, Olympic athlete	David, king***
Charles Bronson, actor	Harpo Marx, comedian***
Phil Linz, New York Yankee	

*The glass harmonica **See YouTube ***The stringed harp

not worrying about time or comparing yourself to others, and soon you'll have a small vocabulary all your own, a little stable of riffs. Good improvisers don't spontaneously come up with new material every time they improvise a solo; they play based on whatever they've learned from past experience and apply it to the situation at hand. Often improvisation is simply a matter of varying a familiar phrase or song a little bit. Create your own little playbook of patterns or phrases—little musical phrases that you like. Experiment with them

HARMONICA *lesson* #27

····⟩ **IF YOU'RE INTIMIDATED,** and if you are still underestimating yourself, I have another idea. Start with these four notes:

3   3   4   4
↑   ↓   ↑   ↓

Played in that order in a certain rhythm, they come out as "Oh When the Saints." Played slow and mournful, they are a wailing gospel blues, like "You've Got to Move." Just keep experimenting with these four notes over a few days, or until your roommate throws a shoe at you. Sometimes having a limit like this helps us to be more creative because we have to do a lot with a little to keep ourselves interested. Think of 3 blow as home base and 4 draw as a satellite base. Three draw and 4 blow are stops along the way. Climb up and down. Skip one or two of the notes. Music, it can be said, is about creating and then resolving tension. Three blow is where the tension is relieved (woo hoo!). Go away from it, stay a while, and then come back. Now you're jamming. Take chances. Go skydiving (an idea that terrifies me) in your mind. Set out on foot for Canada (or if you're already there, for Mexico). Then come back. Guess what— if you just played around with that riff above, you were improvising in cross harp position, so that was a bonus.

until you own them. Keep building your repertoire, adding some new element every now and then—a different rhythm applied to the same notes, a new riff stolen from an old song. As you do this, don't think too hard, and whatever you do, don't invite Mrs. Nelson—the evil piano teacher from your childhood who beat the joy of music out of you—into your head.

When we play music we are telling a story. When we improvise we are making the story up on the spot, like we do when we are spontaneously called upon to entertain our children or friends. There are certain types of stories that have been told for a long time, and storytellers often embellish these older tales to give them new life. Listen to recordings of harmonica players. How are they telling a blues story, or a country story, or a Celtic story? Listen and absorb these other styles, then try your hand at a few notes. See if you can begin one, or end one. Join the many voices around you, and give yourself permission to fool around.

Right now, take your harmonica and pretend you are in the Deep South late in the nineteenth century. Play 3 blow. Now, in small steps, move away from that note, note by slow note, and then return to that note, perhaps by reversing your order, or by jumping back to 3 blow. Try to repeat what you just did, but vary it a little—make it better. Keep going. Tell us a story. Make us remember how sad the world is yet how joyous life is. Take us on a journey.

But let's say you've made some time, turned off the phone, and gotten the materials together. You have everything in shape and it's time to make music, develop a new idea for work, or write, or paint a painting, and instead you find yourself making frequent trips to the refrigerator. You're beginning to wonder if you have any talent as you finish off that pint of Ben and Jerry's Chunky Monkey.

That's okay. Just eat the donuts and get to work. Stop waiting for inspiration to arrive. Don't rush to judge what you do. The vast majority of our first efforts are almost always crappy—this is true of everyone, even bona fide geniuses. All that is required of us is that we make the effort. Later on we can take the raw materials we've created and polish them into something worthwhile.

The most crucial aspect of improvisation is playfulness. Have you ever heard a musician who was playing a lead toss in a bit of melody from something familiar and often silly—"Jingle Bells," or "God Save the Queen"—just for the hell of it? Of course they're showing off, but being playful isn't limited to those with great musical prowess. Even as beginners we can bring a spirit of fun to our music and our lives.

Improvising the Regular Way:

1. Get out your harmonicas.
2. Put on a blues album.
3. Try and play along.

Improvising the Playful Way:

1. Slick back your hair and put on a pair of very dark sunglasses—or if you'd prefer, a clown outfit or a tutu. Or put on all three!
2. Carefully lay each of your harmonicas out on a red satin cloth. Or, if you only own one harmonica, maybe you can find some kind of holster for it. When it's time to play, stand before your arrayed harps or strap on the holster and face the iPod like it's high noon.
3. Put on a series of completely different kinds of music, from advertising jingles to blues to Broadway musicals to AC/DC hits to classical, and try playing along with everything. Don't worry if you sound good or not.
4. When you're done, look in the mirror and say this to yourself: "You kick ass." Make sure you mean it.
5. Treat yourself to your favorite food.

CHAPTER 13

❧

OOPS! ♪

The Law of MISTAKES

"Experience is the name everyone gives to their mistakes."
—OSCAR WILDE

I USED TO BE A PRESBYTERIAN MINISTER IN OMAHA, Nebraska, where I spent a lot of time driving to see people in their homes. One day after visiting someone I became convinced that I could find a shortcut through an undeveloped area that would lead to my home. Using my keen sense of direction I turned left, then right, then right, then up a hill, until I became (you guessed it) hopelessly lost. I turned around and did my best to make my way back to where I had started, but nothing looked familiar. It was during this part of my inadvertent adventure that I noticed a sign that said Neale Woods Nature Center. Curious, I turned up the road and parked my car. A little way in was a wooden building, and on the wall were maps of various trails that set out into the woods and fields from that point.

I took one of the shorter walks and I found myself becoming much calmer. I grew up around woods and it always did me good to walk in them. Neale Woods became one of my favorite haunts, one that I found because I made a mistake.

Every few seconds I make a mistake. When I type, I hit the wrong key, and when I'm not making typos, I'm misspelling words. When I am learning a song I make the same mistakes over and over, as if I am destined to play these wrong notes, and never the right ones.

We all make **mistakes.**
But excessive fear of making mistakes holds us back, and holding back makes us boring.

If you want proof, listen to politicians making speeches—many are so frightened that they say nothing new or interesting and put their audience to sleep.

Of course we can fix many of our mistakes. We can check our writing for errors and correct them. We can go over the hard parts of the song we are learning, slowly and carefully playing them until we have trained the mistakes out of our performance. That's what practice is about. And while we're at it we can be more forgiving of ourselves, recognizing that everyone makes an error now and then, that it is human to do so.

HARMONICA *lesson* #28

····> LET'S SAY WE ARE PLAYING "MARY HAD A LITTLE LAMB":

5	4	4	4	5	5	5
↑	↓	↑	↓	↑	↑	↑
Ma-	ry	had	a	lit-	tle	lamb

But we make a mistake:

5	4	4	4	5	5	6
↑	↓	↑	↓	↑	↓	↑

Now, we could just say we hit a clunker. Or we can decide that we have created a variation on the theme to "Mary Had a Little Lamb." Or perhaps we have the beginnings of an entirely new song about Betty and her little goat. If we see it this way, then we gained something through our error.

But there is another way to look at our mistakes. Sometimes they can bear fruit. Sometimes it is the errors we make that lead to new discoveries. These are happy accidents, and they are part of the magic of creativity.

Many great ideas are discovered by accident when someone makes a mistake. Silly Putty and whole continents have been discovered by mistake. The legendary jazz trumpeter and bandleader Miles Davis had a great attitude about mistakes. "Do not fear mistakes," he said. "There are none." Easy for Miles to say; he was a legendary musician. I've also heard it mentioned that Davis said if a musician didn't make any mistakes in a performance, they "must not have been trying to do anything very interesting."

That sounds about right to me. Stop worrying about being perfect and not making mistakes.

Give yourself a chance to do something interesting.

CHAPTER 14

꙰

Plays Well with Others

"I hold the world but as the world, Gratiano;
A stage where every man must play a part."
—WILLIAM SHAKESPEARE

AL ESCHER TELLS ME THAT WHEN HE WAS GROWING up in Santa Monica back in the 1930s and '40s he had a harmonica teacher named Mr. Luiso. Mr. Luiso was a harmonica booster of the old school, and one of the ways he followed his dream was by encouraging children to join Luiso's harmonica band. Each kid was taught a simple part, and the result was something like a marching band playing John Philip Sousa music, only on a bunch of harmonicas. (I guess Mr. Luiso was sort of like Robert Preston in *The Music Man*.)

As Al remembers it, the band's big event that year was Santa Monica's annual Pioneer Day Parade down Ocean Avenue. The day of the parade, young Al was excited by the pageantry of the day: the flags everywhere, the costumed majorettes, the veterans in uniform, the other marching bands with their brass instruments, and the elegant parade horses in their plumed finery. Mr. Luiso and his harmonica band took their place at the very rear of the entire parade. When the signal came, they all started marching and playing. Everything went great for a while, until Al noticed that his feet were sinking into something squishy, which seemed odd on a day with blue skies on Ocean Avenue in Santa Monica. He looked down and saw to his surprise that he had stepped in a big pile of horse dung. Al was a good band member and started marching again, but now he was worried, because when you are marching along playing the harmonica, the one area you can't see is where you are stepping, and he didn't want to step in any more horse droppings. Out of the corner of his eye he saw other members of the band stumbling and looking down, and from this evidence and the smell, it soon became clear that Luiso's Harmonica Band was marching through a minefield of horse poop.

This might be seen as a good metaphor for life. Or not. There is a lesson here, which is that if you're in a harmonica marching band following horses in a parade, you should watch out for horse poop. And while it is true that sometimes playing with other people can be a crappy experience (har har), most of the time it is worth the reward, and often it is absolutely wonderful.

If you can find the right kind of people—open-minded sorts who aren't snobs or control freaks—one of the most fun things in the world to do is to make music in a group setting. Some of my fondest memories are of singing folk songs with my family and friends, or my sister Katy teaching me "We Are Soldiers in the Army" as we drove

Interesting Quotes About the Harmonica

❉ ❉ ❉ ❉ ❉ ❉ ❉ ❉ ❉ ❉

"The harmonica is a great instrument." —TOOTS THIELEMANS

"I play the harmonica. The only way I can play is if I get my car going really fast, and stick it out the window." —STEPHEN WRIGHT

"I put a new engine in my car but forgot to take the old one out. Now my car goes five hundred miles per hour. The harmonica sounds amazing." —STEPHEN WRIGHT

"I went to the midnight release for the Guitar Hero game and there were less than ten people there. I got the game, but I also got a Guitar Hero Collectible Harmonica! Except, it's out of tune and it was less than a dollar to make . . . but I still got a harmonica! Is anyone jealous?" —ANONYMOUS

"The sole meaning of life is to play harmonica." —LEO TOLSTOY

"How is it possible to play the harmonica professionally for thirty years and still show no sign of improvement?" —MUSIC CRITIC DAVID SINCLAIR ON BOB DYLAN

"Th'Harmonica shall join the sacred choir,
Fresh transports kindle, and new joys inspire
Hark! the soft warblings, sounding smooth and clear,
Strike with celestial ravishment the ear."
—NATHANIEL EVANS, UPON HEARING BENJAMIN FRANKLIN PLAY THE GLASS HARMONICA, WHICH REALLY ISN'T THE SAME INSTRUMENT, BUT HEY . . .

┄┄⟩

INTERESTING QUOTES ABOUT
THE HARMONICA (continued) ♪

❋ ❋ ❋ ❋ ❋ ❋ ❋ ❋ ❋ ❋

"That harmonica don't sound quite right either." —ENNIS DEL MAR IN
BROKEBACK MOUNTAIN

to summer camp, or banging bongos with my brother Dave and his high-school buddies late into the night (or at least until I fell asleep). I remember my brother Phil showing me how to play boogie-woogie on the piano. Later on I accompanied guitarist Preston Reed on harmonica playing little mini-sets in between comedians at the Holy City Zoo in San Francisco, and over the years I played in numerous wannabe rock star bands in seamy bars around New York City, Los Angeles, and in San Francisco. I went to the San Francisco Folk Music Club at Faith Petric's house and played and sang through the night. I sang in church choirs and gospel bands with Burns Stanfield, Dan Fowler, and Steve Horner in Boston, San Francisco, and Omaha. Today I play with the band Los Train Wreck in San Francisco, helping lead the All-Star Jam for all comers, and with the all-author rock band the Rock Bottom Remainders, which raises money for good causes. And through all this, I never once stepped in horse poop.

My income for a lifetime of playing minus expenses might be enough to buy a used car and drive from San Francisco to Fresno and back again several times. Music has not been my path to fame and riches—usually unrealistic goals to expect from our

HARMONICA *lesson* #29

···> **HERE'S A SIMPLE HORN-TYPE LINE.** Play it as four fairly fast, punchy notes of equal length. Try articulating the single notes from the back of your mouth, where you say "kuh":

1   2   3   3
↓   ↑   ↑   ↑

Try hitting the third and forth notes sharply in rapid succession, twice as fast as you play the first two. Try it again, only now hold the fourth note for several beats. Experiment with other rhythms, using these and other notes in simple groupings of a few notes.

Now here's a simple chord rhythm. Remember that chords call for a different-shape mouth. Put the harmonica in front of your two front teeth, wrap your lips around it, and play these chords:

123   123   123   123   ETC.
↓   ↓   ↑   ↑

After you get used to playing this, try putting the accent on the first chord of each pair and play it for about twice as long as the second of each pair. In other words, count two steady beats ("one, two") for the first draw chord and one beat ("three") for the second draw chord, do the same for the two blow chords, and repeat over and over. Keep the counting nice and steady and give yourself time to learn before speeding it up. This creates a rhythm that's often called a shuffle. Famous examples of shuffles are songs like "Kansas City" or Jimmy Reed's "Bright Lights, Big City."

musicianship—but I have had an amazing amount of fun playing with and getting to know many interesting and talented people.

Another important aspect of playing with others is that it allows us to become a part of a larger whole, which is one of life's most rewarding experiences. On harmonica, this is where learning to play rhythmic chords comes in, as well as fills and horn lines. Traditionally a fill (as in filling in), or break, is when the drums play a short solo to signal the beginning of a chorus, verse, or section change, or to highlight something in the music, such as important lyrics. But all instruments can play this role, including the harmonica. A horn line (not the marching band kind) is a catchy, tight, driving, often repeated series of notes played by the horn section of a band. You might know these from rhythm and blues or funk styles of music, like James Brown. When you are playing horn lines or fill, it

HARMONICA *lesson* #30

···♪ Another good technique for blending with a band is playing using "octaves." Put the harmonica deep enough in your mouth that you are playing the bottom four notes simultaneously. Now, lightly rest the tip of your tongue against holes 2 and 3 (feel the ridge at the center lightly pressing against your tongue), and then allow your breath to pass around the sides of your tongue. The goal is to play holes 1 and 4 only—if you do, it will sound something like one note on an accordion. This is because these two holes blow, or draw, produce an octave—on a C harmonica, a C and the next-higher C when you blow, and a D and the next-higher D when you draw. Below is a common riff you can play using octaves. This can sound cool as something you play in between lyrical lines, or as a backup to lyrics, as fill:

1-4   2-5   3-6
 ↓   ↑   ↑

is important to understand that often the most musical choice is to play very sparsely, and at times to lay out altogether. It's good to have an arranger, but it is also good for every musician to think like an arranger—in other words, to have big ears.

So often in life I've wished I had kept my mouth shut and my ears open, but instead I did the reverse, and the results, all too often, were needless fights, embarrassment, and misunderstandings. In one case I unintentionally wound up being elected to student council. In life, as in music, it's good to have big ears.

Rhythmic-style playing can really add a lot to music if done tastefully. Often the members of a band are called upon to vamp for singers or other instruments—that is, to bite their necks or, failing that, to play simple accompaniment or variations of a tune while someone solos, sings, or talks over them. You can do this on your harmonica by playing the two simple chords on page 129 (in and then out) while bouncing your tongue lightly off the roof your mouth. Also, try slapping your tongue on and off the harmonica while you're playing and see what interesting sounds you can make. (Really—I'm not just making you do silly things for the heck of it. I swear!) The action of your tongue combined with the in and out of your breath can provide some terrific rhythmic accompaniment to support the other musicians you're playing with, or they can stand alone. Listen to recordings of Sonny Terry playing with his partner, Brownie McGhee, to get some ideas and inspiration.

When playing a supportive role, remember less is more (or more is less)—this sort of playing is not necessarily desirable through the entire verse of a tune. Once the rhythm is established it can be more effective for the harmonica to play the melody for a few notes, then drop back down to a vamp again before the momentum of the rhythm begins to fade. The main point is to be a good member of the team so that the whole is larger than the sum of the parts.

Some of these are fairly advanced techniques, so don't expect yourself to be able to do everything all at once—no one ever does, and anyhow, you'll need some time to put the pieces together and make it into your music. You need to absorb ideas, listen, and try playing over time to get the whole picture. And, while you're learning and experimenting in this way, it may be that you'll invent something entirely original. Such things often happen by accident—though really it's no accident, because it wouldn't happen if you weren't exploring.

You can learn a lot about playing with other people by listening to and playing along with recorded music, and I encourage you to do that. But there is nothing quite like playing live with real people. Seek out other musicians. Place an ad. Go to open mic nights and jam sessions. Start your own jam sessions. Find folk and traditional music clubs in your area. If you have family and friends who play, work up some songs with them. Houses of worship, camps, and community groups are all good resources. Don't let shyness keep you from having the fun of playing with others.

If on occasion you find yourself stepping in horse poop, don't despair—it just means there's a parade around, somewhere.

CHAPTER 15

Failure *IS* an OPTION

"I spent hours and hours and hours trying to come up with a clever quotation for the beginning of this chapter, but I failed."
—SAM BARRY

MY MOST FABULOUS FAILURE ON THE HARMONICA happened years ago when I was asked to play for a San Francisco avant-garde art group called the Noe Oratorio Society. We were performing a piece by the modern composer Phyllis Tate called "Apparitions," a setting of ghost poems for tenor voice, chromatic harmonica, string quartet, and piano. To me, "Apparitions" sounds something like random notes played by a cat wandering over a piano keyboard, which made the music hard to learn. To make matters worse, there was a long stretch in the middle that called for nothing but the harmonica and the tenor going it alone.

The singer was a handsome fellow with a lovely voice. We met once in his apartment to practice, but we spent most of the time chatting. I did practice quite a bit leading up to the performance, but I was all alone, without the other musicians or a recording. On the night of the show we stood backstage and the tenor turned to me, saying, "I'm relying on you to help me find my way through that section."

This was when I realized how much trouble I was in, because I didn't really know the piece. We were doomed. When the rest of the ensemble stopped playing and left the two of us naked in front of the assembled throng of fifty or so people, we quickly became lost. Both of us gamely pretended we were performing the music as written, but we weren't, and it showed. I was reduced to playing random notes, something like a cat wandering over a keyboard, and the singer was looking for the exit signs. Our effort was a complete sham, and I was very much to blame. It was painfully embarrassing.

That night I learned something: stay away from the Phyllis Tate numbers. And I learned never to agree to do a job unless I was committed to finding a way to make it work. My heart wasn't in it. "Failure is not an option," some cry. Yet we learn more by failure than almost any other experience.

If failure is unavoidable, what then can we do when it comes? How do we avoid the dangers of cynicism and pessimism that threaten to swamp us before we learn something useful and even positively life-changing? Xanax.

Somewhere along the way when we play, we will produce some sound that is objectionable. We'll hit a bad note at a crucial moment or we'll stumble through a piece we thought was polished, or we'll play a very weak bit of improvisation. This happens to everyone.

If we can remember that *every* human fails many times at numerous things, and if we face our failures directly, what appears to be a

🎵

✖ ✖ ✖ ✖ ✖ ✖ ✖ ✖ ✖ ✖

HARMONICA *lesson* #31

⋯⟩ **IN THE SPIRIT OF** celebrating failure and other difficult moments, let's learn the beautiful military funeral and lights-out song, "Taps":

3	3	4	3	4	5			
↑	↑	↑	↑	↑	↑			

3	4	5	3	4	5	3	4	5
↑	↑	↑	↑	↑	↑	↑	↑	↑

4	5	6	5	4	3	3	3	4
↑	↑	↑	↑	↑	↑	↑	↑	↑

If you like, repeat those last three notes, like an echo. Now let's try playing "Taps" in cross harp, which means we'll be playing it in a different key on the same harmonica ("G" on a "C" harp, for instance). This is a little harder, but it's a really good exercise for learning those low draw notes, which is important:

1	1	2	1	2	3			
↓	↓	↓	↓	↓	↓			

1	2	3	1	2	3	1	2	3
↓	↓	↓	↓	↓	↓	↓	↓	↓

2	3	4	3	2	1	1	1	2
↓	↓	↓	↓	↓	↓	↓	↓	↓

dead end can actually lead to new openings. Instead of looking away, we should look straight at the failure and ask questions: Why did I fail? How can I make it easier or better? Why am I a complete and total loser? What does the harmonica have to do with any of this?

Changing our attitude is a key element to finding success in apparent failure. Forgive yourself, count your blessings, and move on. That night when I failed to play well with the Noe Oratorio Society I learned something: If you're going to play, play because you love it. Do what you love—and don't worry about what's in style or what you think somebody else thinks you should be doing. Play the music you love, or play for people you love, or better yet, do both.

If At First You Don't Succeed,
MAYBE YOU SHOULD QUIT WHILE YOU'RE AHEAD

- Bill Gates was a dropout whose first business venture was a flop. He went on to found a company that many people consider to be the root of all evil.

- Walt Disney's first commercial effort failed. Deeply embittered, he created Disneyland, a nightmarish fantasy world where people stand in endless lines while being badgered by cartoon figures with giant heads.

- 1912: The *Titanic* hit an iceberg, killing actor Leonardo DiCaprio.

- Matt Damon dropped out of Harvard University twelve credits short of earning his degree. The message? Matt, there's still time to finish your education.

- Abraham Lincoln and Lucille Ball's partnership began with a spectacular failure when their Vitametavegimin vitamin syrup business went bankrupt. This was followed by an equally fabulous success when they invented the first affordable desktop computer, affectionately known as the Macintosh. Tragically, Lucille Ball was assassinated by the insanely jealous Bill Gates.

CHAPTER 16

ETIQUETTE

Good Manners Matter

"You can't be truly rude until you understand good manners."
—RITA MAE BROWN

EVERYONE WAS EXCITED. WE WERE THERE TO HEAR A great band. The lights dimmed and the crowd quieted. We saw the silhouette of a figure onstage and everyone cheered, but then we realized it was a member of the stage crew. Then the lights came up, the band came out, we went wild, and they began to play. When Kermit sang that duet with Miss Piggy, I was transported beyond all reason.

No, seriously, I was seeing a real band made up of actual human beings. The house was rocking that night, and I had a great seat, front row, stage left, listening to one of my favorite bands. I was getting lost in the moment when something jarring entered my consciousness—a note was off. A moment later I was able to identify the sounds as a harmonica, but no one in the band was playing one. I looked around and saw a man wailing on his harp as loud as he could, as though he were part of the band. He wasn't playing that well and I'm not sure he was even playing in the right key, but even if he had been, this man was being extraordinarily rude.

In this book I have urged you not to worry about what other people think of you, but we all need to have good manners. We should never let insecurity rule the day, but now I want to talk about the ways in which we *should* be concerned with other people's feelings.

Let's face it: when someone shows off, whether it's vacation photos, an expensive new car, new breast implants, or a newfound skill, it can be downright irritating to everyone else if it's done without tact or awareness. There's a saying—just because you can doesn't mean you should. Blowing your horn in an annoying manner doesn't gain you any friends, and it may even alienate people. There's a time and a place to strut your stuff, but there's never a time when modesty and tact aren't appropriate.

You may have noticed that I brought up the subject of the harmonica several times in this book. (You may have also noticed that I brought up the love of my life—Miss Piggy.) As with all creative endeavors, playing the harmonica should be done tastefully, or at least in a manner in keeping with the setting. But too many players think that because they have a harp in their pocket they can just start wailing away whenever and wherever they want. (It *is* okay, however, to play in Saint Patrick's Cathedral.) These people should be tied in a chair and forced to listen to a reading of the tax code.

You may not be this kind of person. In fact, you may be too shy

THE HARMONICA INCIDENT:
AUGUST 20, 1964

⋯⟩ Harmonica players everywhere owe a deep debt of gratitude to intrepid sportswriter Harvey Frommer for uncovering the truth about what has become known as "The Harmonica Incident." On August 20, 1964, a harmonica was used as a weapon on the New York Yankees' team bus, leading to a wide-ranging baseball scandal and the end of Yogi Berra's career as the Yankees manager. Well, maybe not quite, but something happened.

That year Yogi Berra had succeeded Ralph Houk as skipper, but there were reports that his players didn't take him entirely seriously in the role. (People having trouble taking Yogi Berra seriously. Go figure.) The mighty Bronx Bombers had won four straight pennants, but most of the 1964 season had been a disappointment. In late August the team was hovering in third place behind Baltimore and Chicago. They had just lost four straight games to the White Sox and were on the team bus heading to O'Hare Airport, demoralized.

A reserve infielder named Phil Linz—a career .235 hitter who was still not entirely accepted in the Yankees team culture—was sitting in the back of the bus, which was stuck in heavy traffic. It was a hot, humid summer day.

"I was bored," Linz said. "I pulled out my harmonica. I had the learner's sheet for 'Mary Had a Little Lamb.' So I started fiddling. You blow in. You blow out." (A brilliant observation on Linz's part. Maybe he should have written this book? Too late! Ha ha!)

Berra, under stress as the manager of a third-place team that

⋯⟩

The Harmonica Incident
(continued)

was expected to win the pennant in an easy stroll, snapped from the front of the bus, "Knock it off!" When Linz asked what their manager had said, Mickey Mantle replied, "Play it louder," and Linz obliged.

Berra stomped to the back of the bus, saying, "Shove that thing."

"I told Yogi that I didn't lose that game," Linz recalled. In response, Berra smacked the harmonica out of Linz's hands. It flew into Joe Pepitone's knee and Pepitone jokingly winced in pain. Soon the entire bus—except for Berra—was in stitches (while Pepitone needed them).

Linz was fined $200. "The next day," Linz says, "the Hohner Company called and I got a contract for $5,000 to endorse their harmonica. The whole thing became a big joke."

The incident may have changed the season for the Yankees. The Yankees had a 22-6 record in September and won the pennant in a close race with the White Sox. A World Series loss to the St. Louis Cardinals in seven games cost Berra his job, but according to Harvey Frommer, there were those who said he was on his way out the day of the "Harmonica Incident."

about playing. I don't want you to be too shy—I want you to be like Miss Piggy. I also want you to know when it's appropriate to play so you can play with confidence. First of all, remember to ask the other musicians if it's okay to join in. Even if it's a jam session with longer solos, we should always be courteous, listen to others, and take turns. Basically, use common sense and courtesy, and you should be okay. There's a place for you to shine, but you don't want to force your playing on people when it may not be appropriate.

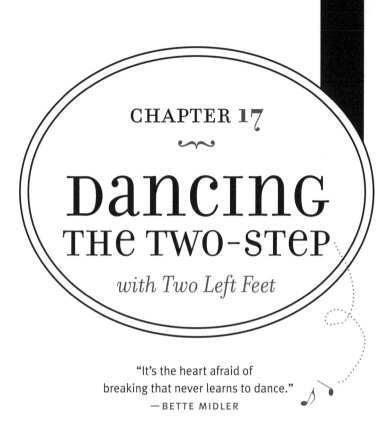

CHAPTER 17

DANCING
THE TWO-STEP

with Two Left Feet

"It's the heart afraid of
breaking that never learns to dance."
—BETTE MIDLER

I AM NOT A GOOD DANCER. It's possible that I have it in me, but when it comes to dancing I seem to be unable to practice what I am preaching in this book. Somewhere along the way I let my dancing feet wither on the vine, which seems to be a mixed metaphor. I went from being open to the idea that I could learn to dance, way back when, to convincing myself that I couldn't, because I couldn't *yet*. There's a world of difference between "I can't" and "I can't *yet*," and if we're not careful, a pessimistic outlook can quickly become our permanent reality if we don't resist its seductive charm.

So I decided to fight back. Well, actually, I decided to dance back.

One night I was at a legendary Austin, Texas, country music club called the Broken Spoke with Kathi and I knew she wanted to dance. I've already made it clear that I'm not much of a dancer, right? And I sure didn't know how to dance the country two-step. But I screwed up my courage, asked Kathi for a dance, and the next thing you knew we were out there on the floor.

Okay, it wasn't like the movies. The other dancers didn't form a circle around us and marvel at our grace. Kathi showed me the basics, and we started moving in a counter-clockwise direction with everyone else. Some of the other dancers were durn good (this is how I talk when I'm in Texas). They whirled and twirled past us, smilin' as they showed off their moves.

Meanwhile, Kathi and I were making pretty good headway, though Kathi kept softly counting "one-two-one-two-one-two" to keep us in line. I started to enjoy myself a little. I was doing it—I was dancing! Round and round we went, "one-two-one-two" through a couple of songs. It was even beginning to seem easy, though I did tend to fall off the count every couple of feet.

Then, all of a sudden, with a jolt we banged directly into another couple. And not just any other couple—one of the star dance couples. It was quite a collision, but everyone recovered their balance and exchanged polite apologies. Then away they went, whirling and twirling.

"That wasn't our fault," I murmured indignantly in Kathi's ear. It seemed to me we had been perfectly within our rights to be where we had been when the accident occurred.

"Maybe not," Kathi responded, "but we're the only ones out here who are counting out loud."

HARMONICA *lesson* #32

···⟩ **TRY PLAYING THIS OLD GOSPEL BLUES,** "You've Got to Move," which might be more familiar as a song performed by the Rolling Stones. (Find it and give a listen.) Focus on playing single notes, and on the two bent notes a light "tuh" action with the tongue might help you get the lower pitch. Here goes:

3	3	4	4
↑	↓	↑	↓
You've got	to	move	

4	4	3	3
↓	↓	↑	↓
You've got	to	move	

4	4	4	4	4
↓	↓	↓	↓	↑
You've got	to	move, child		

3	3	3	3
↑	↗̸	↗̸	↑
You've got	to	move	

1	2	3	3	3	3-2-1
↓	↑	↑	↓	↓	↑-↑-↓
'Cause when the	Lord	gets	ready		

2	3	2	3
↑	↑	↑	↑
You've got	to	move	

"YOU'VE GOT TO MOVE"

Overall it was a victory for me that night. I danced and I had fun. I can't tell you that I've gone on to enroll in a dance school, though periodically I threaten to. But at least I tried it, and I mean to try it again sometime. No longer can I say, "I can't dance." Because now I know that I can, if I want to. ("One-two-one-two-one-two . . .") All it took was the willingness to try.

If you keep working at something and don't give up, before you know it you'll be an old pro. I may not be a good dancer—yet—but when I play one of my old harps, I feel I know what it would be like to be Fred Astaire, to be able to move my body with complete confidence. On the harmonica I can whirl and twirl better than that couple we collided with on that Austin dance floor. Playing has added immeasurably to my life. And all because my brother handed me a harmonica and I took it on a walk in the woods.

Keep playing and listening, and before you know it, you and your harmonicas will be old, comfortable friends. You will have your own unique sound—every player I've ever known does.

Life is a precious gift. A playful spirit makes life infinitely more joyful for you and for those around you.

Soon you'll be saying, "I know how to play."
Because you do.